Frederic George Stephens

Dante Gabriel Rossetti

Frederic George Stephens

Dante Gabriel Rossetti

ISBN/EAN: 9783337077068

Printed in Europe, USA, Canada, Australia, Japan

Cover: Foto ©Thomas Meinert / pixelio.de

More available books at **www.hansebooks.com**

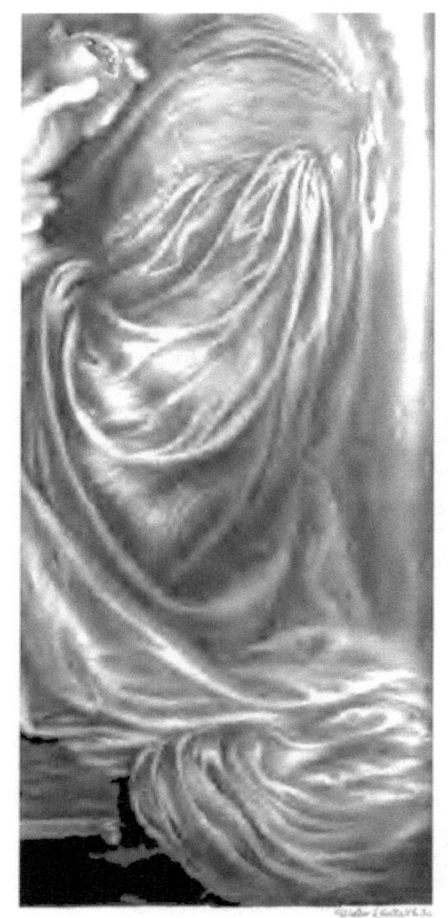

Proserpine

DANTE GABRIEL ROSSETTI

By

F. G. STEPHENS

Author of "Flemish Relics," "Landseer," etc.

LONDON
SEELEY AND CO. LIMITED, ESSEX STREET, STRAND
NEW YORK, MACMILLAN AND CO.
1894

LIST OF ILLUSTRATIONS

PLATES.

	PAGE
Proserpine . . . . *Frontispiece*	
Dante on the Anniversary of Beatrice's Death . . . . *to face*	34
Found	38
Venus Verticordia	64

ILLUSTRATIONS IN THE TEXT.

Genevieve. Rossetti's First complete Design.	16
"Ecce Ancilla Domini!"	20
The Laboratory	26
Pages Quarrelling	28
D. G. Rossetti	29
How they met Themselves	33
The Artist's Wife	37
Margaret and Faust	43
The San Grael	44
Study for Guinevere and Sir Lancelot	46
Study for Guinevere	47
Ancilla San Grael	48
Lancelot in Guinevere's Chamber	49
Alma Mater and Mr. Woodward	50

ILLUSTRATIONS IN THE TEXT

	PAGE
Dante	51
Girl plucking Fruit	52
Lucrezia Borgia	53
Dr. Johnson at the Mitre	55
Paolo and Francesca da Rimini	59
Study of a Head	63
Lilith	67
The Lady with the Chain	71
Our Lady of Pity	76
Lady with a Fan	79
Sancta Lilias, which was founded on The Blessed Damozel	87
Two Figures Embracing, from The Blessed Damozel	89
The Sphinx	91
Christina Rossetti	93
Beatrice and her Nurse	94

DANTE GABRIEL ROSSETTI

PAINTER AND POET

CHAPTER I

1828—1851.

Nowhere in Time's vista, where the forms of great men gather thickly, do we see many shapes of those who, as painters and as poets have been alike illustrious. Among the few to whom, equally on both accounts, conspicuous honours have been paid, none is superior to Rossetti, of whose genius doubly exalted the artists say that in design he was pre-eminent, while, on the other hand, the most distinguished poets of our age place him in the first rank with themselves. As to this prodigious, if not unique, distinction, of which the present age has not yet, perhaps, formed an adequate judgment, there can be no doubt that with regard to the constructive portion of his genius Rossetti was better equipped in verse than in design.

It is certain that our subject looked upon himself rather as a painter who wrote than as a verse-maker who painted. It is probable that the very facility, which, of course, had been won with enormous pains, and was maintained with characteristic energy and constant care, of his literary efforts led Rossetti to slightly undervalue the rare gifts of which his pen was the instrument, while, as to painting, his hard-won triumphs with design, colour, expression, form, and visible beauty of all sorts seemed to him the aptest as well as the most successful exponents of the passionate poetry it was, by one means or the other, his object to make manifest. His mission was that of a poet in art as in verse, and, by devoting the greater part of his life and all his more arduous efforts to the former means, he made it plain that, notwithstanding all obstacles, the palette served his purpose better than the pen. I refer thus emphatically to Rossetti's genius in its double form as well as to the inevitable division of his energies which attended that circumstance, because, while I wonder at his achievements and know how great were the powers he employed, I cannot help thinking that a less complex nature than his would have done still more than, so far as time and space allow, these pages have to report of and illustrate.

Gabriel Charles Dante was the elder son, and, his sister Maria Francesca being his senior, the second child of Gabriele Rossetti and Frances Mary Lavinia, his wife, born Polidori; she wrote some essays and educational books of value, and died several years ago. William Michael, third child of this union (born in 1829), is the still living accomplished writer on poetry and art, and the tenant of a high post in the Inland Revenue Department, Somerset House. The fourth child is Miss Christina Georgina Rossetti (born 1830) whose *Goblin Market* attests her to be one of the most distinguished poetesses of this century. Gabriele Rossetti was descended from an Italian family of good standing, whose original name was Della Guardia, and he was born in 1783 at Vasto d'Ammone, in the Abruzzi, the son of one Nicola, who was connected with the iron trade of that town. Gabriele, a man of culture, whose specialty was in profound studies of Dante—whence one of the names of his elder son—removed to Naples, and held an honourable office as custodian of antique bronzes in the then Bourbon Museum of the capital. This post and all his other possessions were forfeited in 1821, when he joined in revolutionary movements against Ferdinand I., King of the Two Sicilies, which, by the aid of the Austrians, were defeated and the chiefs proscribed. Among them Rossetti took refuge at Malta in 1822, and, ultimately, in London, where he arrived in 1825, and in the next year married the above-named lady, who was a daughter of Signor Gaetano Polidori, a secretary of Count Alfieri, the Italian poet and supposed second husband of Louisa of Stolberg, Countess of Albany, wife and widow of Charles Edward Stuart, the besotted Young Pretender. The wife of Signor Gaetano was a Miss Pierce, an Englishwoman. Besides the lady who became Mrs. Gabriele Rossetti, Gaetano had for his son Dr. Polidori, one of Lord

Byron's physicians, with whom his lordship fell foul in a certain *Epistle to Mr. Murray*, and who, with other things in verse and prose, wrote a sanguinary novelette called *The Vampire*, which still retains its shadow of a reputation. Arrived in London Gabriele Rossetti maintained himself as a teacher of his native tongue, and succeeded so well in that capacity that the Professorship of Italian in King's College was offered to him and accepted in 1831.

As might be expected of one possessing so many accomplishments and whose career had been marked by so much courage, the professor was a man of striking character and aspect, so that when I was introduced to him in 1848, and his grand climacteric was past, and, as with most Italians, a life of studies told upon him heavily, I could not but be struck by the noble energy of his face and by the high culture his expression attested, while a sort of eager, almost passionate, resolution seemed to glow in all he said and did. To a youngster, such as I was then, he seemed much older than his years, and while seated reading at a table with two candles behind him and, because his sight was failing, with a wide shade over his eyes, he looked a very Rembrandt come to life. The light was reflected from a manuscript placed close to his face, and, in the shadow which covered them, made distinct all the fineness and vigour of his sharply moulded features. It was half lost upon his somewhat shrunken figure wrapped in a student's dressing-gown, and shone fully upon the lean, bony, and delicate hands in which he held the paper. He looked like an old and somewhat imperative prophet, and his voice had a slightly rigorous ring speaking to his sons and their visitors. Near his side, but beyond the radiant circle of the candles—her erect, comely, and very English form, and face remarkable for its noble and beautiful matronhood, and but half visible in the flickering glow of the fire—sat Mrs. Rossetti, the mother of Dante Gabriel. He too, leaning his elbows upon the table and holding his face between both hands so that the long curling masses of his dark brown hair fell forward, sat on the other side, his attenuated features sharply outlined by the candle's light.

It is certain that the scene which thus impressed my memory was not presented at No. 38, Charlotte Street, Portland Place, one of those then very "respectable," but dull, and now much deteriorated opposing lines of brick walls, with rectangular holes in them, which Londoners call houses, where, on the 12th of May, 1828, our subject was born; it was No. 50 in the same street which was thus signalised. To the latter house the Rossetti family migrated about the time in question. It is fortunate that a "Board" has not yet, as in many neighbouring regions, changed the numbers of the houses in Charlotte Street, and that its monkey-like activity has, for the present at least, spared the record of a famous family. Nevertheless, the birthplace of the Rossettis will, doubtless, some day be marked with an honourable white stone. Certain it is that they were all born at No. 38, and that in April, 1854, and at another house in Albany Street, the ardent self-sacrificing patriotism of Professor Gabriele Rossetti found its earthly close. Tennyson's "long unlovely" Wimpole Street, where the Laureate was wont to stand waiting for the

"hand that can be clasped no more,"

and which is close to our poet's birthplace, is not more "bald," than that which took its name from the ill-favoured wife of George III. Rossetti was christened Charles after Mr. Charles Lyell, his godfather, of Kinnordy, Fife (whose more famous son wrote *The Principles of Geology*), Gabriel, after his father, and Dante after the illustrious poet. We know that his first teaching was due to his mother, an accomplished and devoted matron whose affection was, even to his latest days, ceaselessly acknowledged by her son. Mr. Knight tells us the lad's first school was under the Rev. Mr. Paul, in Foley Street, whence, in 1837, he was with his brother, removed to King's College School, where he stayed till 1843, and received all the advantages of that capital academy; these, however, did not include what are now called "sports," a circumstance which of course had not a little influence on his character in after life.[1]

At King's College School the Italian professor's son acquired, as his brother tells us, "an education in Latin, French, and the rudiments of

[1] It has been said that Rossetti shared at least some of the athletic proclivities and aptitudes of British youth, and was accustomed to enjoy energetic exercises. This is quite a mistake, for, although he was in youth a tolerably good walker, he never excelled in that respect. It was an error which has made him appear as a rower; indeed, I remember when in my boat he proposed, because it was in his way, to throw overboard one of the stretchers (!); he never cared to swim, and, as he did not ride at all, he could not be called a rider. The fact is that, when he pleased, which, until his later days,

Greek." Italian was, of course, his customary, if not his native tongue; to these collectively considerable attainments must be added a "certain knowledge of German," which was more than enough to enable him to read in that language. After some tentative literary efforts, resulting in an experimental drama, and a prose romance or two, besides a narrative poem which was printed by his grandfather, Mr. Gaetano Polidori, Rossetti determined to become an artist. This was in the autumn of 1843, a date which, however, must not be taken as that of the youth's beginning to draw. Indeed, his brother tells us that our subject was even then a member of a sketching club, and the same authority still possesses some drawings made in ink to illustrate a story of the designer's, called *Sorrentino*, by means of which, by the way, he even thus early appears in that double capacity of author and artist which always obtained with him. The influence of Retzsch and his once-famous *Outlines* anent *Faust* was manifest in all the productions of this category by Rossetti, as well as all his colleagues of the P-R.B. who could draw, that is six of the seven. Every one of these was accustomed to make designs in this manner. Thus, some of the finest "inventions" of Sir John Millais's most brilliant youth were, with stringent care and delicacy, put upon paper. That influence is manifest in the beautiful outlined design called *Genevieve*, which charms us in this text, and has not been reproduced till now.

There is no doubt that Rossetti's systematic training as an artist was begun in 1843, and at Mr. Cary's then well-known academy, which stood at the south-east corner of Charlotte Street and Streatham Street, Bloomsbury. It was a capital drill-ground for drawing from the antique, beyond which step of his training Rossetti did not pass in that place, including drawing from the human skeleton, but not painting. Here, with frequent excursions into the realms of poetry proper, he remained, I fear, in a somewhat desultory mood, rather less than three years, during which period he prepared the drawing of a statue, then demanded by the Royal Academy ere its tyros were admitted as Probationers to the Antique School in Trafalgar Square. In July, 1846, he was admitted a Student of the Academy. "I saw," says a fellow was both often and long, no one worked harder than Rossetti; but, as a glance at his frame and face amply attested, his energy was not physical. In after life he deplored his youthful neglect of school games and struggles of the more manly kind.

student, "Rossetti, whom Fame of a sort had preceded, enter the school with a knot of Probationers, who, as if to keep each other in countenance, herded together. All their forerunners turned, as was natural, to the door of the room, and noticed among the freshmen the saturnine, thin, and for a youth of nearly eighteen, not well-developed tyro other 'Caryites' had talked of as a poet whose verses had been actually printed, and whom they described as a clever sketcher of chivalric and satiric subjects, who, in addition, did all sorts of things in all sorts of unconventional ways. Thick, beautiful, and closely curled masses of rich brown much-neglected hair, fell about an ample brow, and almost to the wearer's shoulders; strong eyebrows marked with their dark shadows a pair of rather sunken eyes, in which a sort of fire, instinct of what may be called proud cynicism, burned with a furtive kind of energy, and was distinctly, if somewhat luridly, glowing. His rather high cheekbones were the more observable because his cheeks were roseless and hollow enough to indicate the waste of life and midnight oil to which the youth was addicted; close shaving left bare his very full, not to say sensuous, lips and square-cut masculine chin. Rather below the middle height, and with a slightly rolling gait, Rossetti came forward among his fellows with a jerky step, tossed the falling hair back from his face, and, having both hands in his pockets, faced the student world with an *insouciant* air which savoured of defiance, mental pride and thorough self-reliance. A bare throat, a falling, ill-kept collar, boots not over familiar with brushes, black and well-worn habiliments, including, not the ordinary frock or jacket 'of the period,' but a very loose dress-coat which had once been new—these were the outward and visible signs of a mood which cared even less for appearances than the art-student of those days was accustomed to care, which undoubtedly was little enough. Apart from all these unconventionalities one saw at a glance that the partial slovenliness of the newcomer was far from being a sign of mere vanity affecting pride and, in contempt for others, seeking to be singular." It must be remembered that Rossetti had all his life been accustomed to meet in his father's house poets, scholars, and patriots of mark. When he entered the Academy he was by no means unknown, many a "Caryite" had preceded him from Bloomsbury, and not a few turned to welcome him to the Antique School.

In that school Rossetti worked somewhat less than was desirable, intermittently, and as if without a serious intention to profit by it to the utmost; nor did he ever pass to the higher grades of the Life and Painting Schools. It is clear that literature, abundant reading and writing poetry were his chief delights till about March, 1848, when, much stirred by the vigorous and noble design of Madox Brown's *The Giaour's Confession*, which was at the Academy in 1841, and *Parisina*, which he saw at the British Institution in 1845, and thus strengthened impressions due to the same fine artist's contributions to the Westminster Hall Exhibitions of 1844 and 1845,[1] and, above all, to the pathos and originality of his works as a whole, he wrote to the latter expressing the highest admiration of his powers, and begged for lessons in painting, in the technique of which our subject had, it is beyond question, made no considerable progress. This appeal was made in such enthusiastic terms that as, with a great deal of humour, Brown was wont to tell in after years, the recipient fancied such compliments were not unlikely to cover an intention to "make fun" of him. Brown therefore, before calling on his would-be pupil, provided himself with a thick stick and sallied forth, intending to use it if need be. To Charlotte Street he went, and seeing "Mr. Rossetti" on the doorplate was partly reassured, but held to the cudgel until the young Rossetti's manifest sincerity disarmed all suspicion and, finally, impelled Brown so warmly that he then and there undertook the office of a teacher, not for fees, but entirely for the love of art, and in order to be helpful to one so anxious and so deeply moved. Rossetti himself was wont gleefully to tell his intimates that the first result of Brown's teaching was dismay, because the subject set before the pupil for accurate and stringent imitation was a group of jars, such as pickle-pots, or some such things, in still life, the uncompromising prose of which did not suit the aspirations of the tyro. Nevertheless, there can be no doubt whatever that to Brown's guidance and example we owe the better part of Rossetti as a painter *per se*, although his will to study with tenacity, and thus command success, might have been stiffened by the encouragement and example of Mr. Holman Hunt, apart from which, I fear the latter-named student was not

[1] These were *The Body of Harold brought to the Conqueror*, a cartoon, 1844, and *Justice*, 1845.

the fittest guide for a genius like Rossetti, who very soon departed from the uncompromising principles of the indomitable friend who had never been, even for an hour, his model in art. Rather had the brilliant and happy power of Millais, one of the truest painters of the age and a born artist, been as light before the subject of these pages. Rossetti was considerably behind his friends. Brown was his senior by seven years, and a thoroughly trained artist, who had exhibited in this country in 1841; Millais was a Gold Medal Student in the Royal Academy before the foundation of the P-R.B., and an exhibitor in 1846; while Mr. Holman Hunt, an exhibitor from the last-named year, had passed through ordeals of practice and training of the most self-exacting stringency, far beyond what Rossetti, although he had never departed from the conviction that his chief function was painting, and not poetry, had submitted to.

Desiring to become a thoroughly trained painter, Rossetti wrote to Brown. It appears that, with greatly increased admiration of Brown's skill and genius, Rossetti, who had seen besides *Parisina*, and other instances at the British Institution, found his impressions strengthened by that artist's contribution to the " Free Exhibition of Modern Art,"[1] which later in the spring of 1848, was formed near Hyde Park Corner. This was *The First Translation of the Bible into English*, or, more aptly, *Wickliffe reading his Translation of the New Testament to John of Gaunt*. Painted in 1847-8, it was No. 216 at the gallery in question, where it attracted much attention, aroused abundant controversies, and, above all, allowing for the idiosyncrasies of the artist, was the first Pre-Raphaelite picture of the original stamp ever produced. It

[1] This gallery was afterwards known as the Portland Gallery, and removed to Regent Street, where it survived till 1861. It was originally held in the *ci-devant* Chinese Gallery, Hyde Park Corner, and filled a long, well-lighted brick building standing on a site in the rear of the present Alexandra Hotel, and originally constructed for the exhibition and sale of Chinese and Japanese *bric à brac*. The time not being ripe for an adequate development of that cult of quaintness and strong colour which has culminated in the wildest Impressionism, so-called, of which we are now witnessing the decline and fall, the Chinese Gallery, as an exhibition, came to grief in a year or two. It gave way to the "Free Exhibition," as it was humorously called, because there was nothing free about it, the artists paying for their places, besides a percentage on the prices of their pictures when they sold them there, while the public paid for the privilege of seeing them as well as for the catalogues which described them.

was, of course, exhibited months before the foundation of the Brotherhood in the autumn of 1848, and undertaken while the P-R.Bs. proper were still in their original darkness. A happy combination of Italian taste, and the technique of the Low Countries of the pre-Rubensian epoch, the gravity, energy, high finish, and pure and brilliant coloration of this noble piece had, as I said in the *Portfolio* of 1893, p. 66, profound effects upon the painters of the Brotherhood.

It was in the autumn of 1848, that Rossetti, finding the accommodation of the paternal house in Charlotte Street too limited for his purpose, joined Mr. Holman Hunt (with whom he had not previously been particularly intimate) in renting a studio at the then No. 7 Cleveland Street, Fitzroy Square, a house which as No. 46 still stands next to the south-west corner of Howland Street, before one reaches the workhouse. It was a dismal place, the one big window of which looked to the east, and through which, when neither smoke, fog, nor rain obscured the unlovely view, you could see the damp, orange-coloured piles of timber a neighbouring dealer in that material had, within a few yards of the room, piled in monstrous heaps upon his backyard. In this very forlorn quarter Rossetti began his first picture in oil that deserved the name, although certain tentative experiments in portraiture with that vehicle had exercised him with more severity than success. Nothing could be more depressing than the large gaunt chamber where the young artist executed two memorable pictures and from which posterity must perforce date the inception of Pre-Raphaelitism of the primitive and stringent, not to say hide-bound sort. Except early in the morning, nothing like that fulness of light which painters now demand was obtainable where the dingy walls, distempered of a dark maroon which dust and smoke stains had deepened, added a most undesirable gloom. The approach to it was by a half-lighted staircase up which the fuss and clatter of a boys' school kept by the landlord of the house, and too often dashed with sounds of chastisement and sorrow, frequently arose; add to these uncomely elements a dimly lighted hall, surcharged by air of which the damp of the timber yard was not the only source of its mustiness, and a shabby out-at-elbows doorway, giving access from the street that, even then, was rapidly "going down in the world." It was sliding so to say, to its present *zero* of rag and bottle shops, penny barbers, pawnbrokers and retailers of the smallest possible capital. Such was the place where Mr. Holman Hunt, then in his twenty-second year, and Rossetti, who had just completed his second decade, met and began to work out their destinies. The former, who on that occasion left his father's house, was the master of a good deal less than a hundred pounds, being the price, or what remained of that sum, for which he had sold to a prize holder of the "Art Union,"[1] his noteworthy No. 804 in the Academy of 1848, entitled *The Flight of Madeline and Porphyro*, an illustration of Keats's *Eve of St. Agnes*. It was an excellent example which, without the least quality of Pre-Raphaelitism, attested the remarkable skill of the artist and his rare sense of the picturesque in design. He had before this time painted, besides pot-boiling portraits, two or three less ambitious works.

Rossetti was yet, apart from the studio, a member of his father's family, and, unlike his comrade, still, being so young, dependent upon his father, but resolutely devoted to art, that is to say to the expression of the poetry of his nature by means of painting, rather than in verse. It is the more to his honour that, while his facility in verse was rare, brilliant, and great, he had at this period to undergo agonies of toil and passionately to, so to say, tear himself to pieces, while he became a painter according to the lofty standards of Madox Brown, Holman Hunt, and John Millais. These, as well as other friends of his, witnessed the greatness of the struggle and honoured accordingly the

---

[1] This was the now deceased Mr. Charles Bridger, a well-known archæologist and antiquary, whose *Index to Printed Pedigrees* has proved the value of his services. The prize was £60 or thereabouts, for the winner being a friend of mine, I negotiated the business, but forget the exact sum in question.

[2] Millais, too, had exhibited at the Academy in 1846, his *Pizarro seizing the Inca of Peru*, his *Elgiva* (which he sold for £120) in 1847; his picture of *The Widow's Mite*, which, with life-size figures, was at Westminster Hall in 1849, occupied this artist in 1848, so that he exhibited nothing at the Academy in that year. There was no Pre-Raphaelitism in any of these instances, nor otherwise until the painters' contributions to the Academy of 1849 marked their adherence to the newly pronounced principles of the Brotherhood. In March of this year Rossetti's *Girlhood of Mary, Virgin* was shown at Hyde Park Corner, and by Brown, his splendid *King Lear*, which is now in the collection of Mr. Leathart, of Gateshead, and, as a powerful illustration of Pre-Raphaelitism a glory of the English School, worthy to be compared with any masterpiece of Rossetti in his riper days, with *A Huguenot*, or *The Proscribed Royalist* of Millais.

victor of that strenuous self-contest. Under these conditions, and in the studio here described Rossetti began to paint *The Girlhood of Mary, Virgin*, which is, so far as he was concerned, the first outcome of the Pre-Raphaelite views he had accepted. Whether he had adopted them under the inspiration of one or more of his friends, or, as some have supposed, had invented them, matters little. That he took an independent line in regard to art the work in question emphatically affirms; the truth seems to be that Brown's influence predominated in his studies, while the mysticism of his own mind directed him where neither the dramatic intensity of Millais and Brown, still less the stringent realism of Mr. Holman Hunt, had any power. The design was, I think, made rather early in 1848, probably before going to Cleveland Street.

How independent that line of thought and art had already become, that is how entirely free from impressions due to any of those artists of power with whom he was then associated, I could not better demonstrate than by setting before the reader a very sufficient, but much reduced transcript of Rossetti's design, made in fine outlines and exquisitely drawn, to illustrate Coleridge's *Love*, and having for its text the wooing of Genevieve—

> "She lean'd against the armed man,
> The statue of the armed knight;
> She stood and listened to my lay,
> Amid the lingering light.
>
> * * * *
>
> I played a soft and doleful air,
> I sang an old and moving story—
> An old rude song, that suited well
> That ruin wild and hoary."

If ever pencil gave the tender pathos and suggested the moving cadences of a poet's verse this lovely drawing, which has never been reproduced before, does so entirely and sympathetically. Quoting his brother's own record, a sort of diary, Mr. W. M. Rossetti tells us that "On August 28 [1848] Rossetti sat up all night, and made, from 11 p.m. till 6 a.m. an outline of Coleridge's *Genevieve*, 'certainly the best thing I have done.'"[1] The drawing was, I believe, produced

---

[1] The choice instance is made in ink, with a very fine, probably crow-quill, pen, and bears, in a monogram, "G. C. D. R., August, 1848." Not long after this the artist ceased

as the artist's contribution to a rather ambitious body calling itself "The Cyclographic Society," of which each member furnished a design to be placed in a portfolio with others, circulated and subjected to the criticism of all those other members who chose to offer their opinions. The design itself was given to Mr. Coventry Patmore who, not long since, gave it to Sir E. Burne-Jones, to be exchanged for a drawing by that master himself. It now belongs to Sir Edward, who generously lent it to illustrate this sketch of his old friend's art.

Genevieve.
Rossetti's first complete Design. Lent by Sir E. Burne-Jones.

To return to *The Girlhood of Mary, Virgin*, the style, gravity, and grace of which are manifest developments of the like qualities of *Genevieve*, it is indispensable to illustrate the leading facts in its history, as the first example of Rossetti as a Pre-Raphaelite out of which naturally arises an account of the origin of the Brotherhood bearing that name. Mr. Holman Hunt has in the *Fortnightly Review* given a version of the history of the body, which, though not quite complete, is, as far as it goes, correct. It is to the effect that some time after the two comrades settled in Cleveland Street, they encountered at Millais's

to use his name of Charles, and thenceforth adopted the style "Dante G. Rossetti," or a monogram, of which there is more than one version, comprising "D. G. R." only.

house in Gower Street, a book of engravings from frescoes in the Campo Santo of Pisa, that is to say from pictures, the purity, energy, simplicity, and poetic veracity of which served as points of crystallisation, or *nuclei* of enthusiasm for the till then somewhat nebulous ideals in art the three men severally and independently of each other possessed. Then and there, or very shortly afterwards, the friends determined to form what may be called a League of Sincerity, with loftier aims than artists generally cared for, a leading principle of which implied that each confessor should paint his best with due reference to nature, without which there could be no sincerity. There was no intention of following, much less copying the modes and moods of the artists who preceded Raphael, nor of rejecting anything which had been attained in art's service since the days of that Prince of Painters. Each friend was to work in his own way, and, if an edifying use could be made of the subject he chose for his art, so much the better, yet nothing like a didactic, religious, or moral purpose was insisted on by any Brother. The enthusiasm of Rossetti prompted the idea of forming a "Brotherhood," which in a very few days was enlarged to include James Collinson, then a painter of domestic *genre* of conspicuous ability and great promise; Thomas Woolner, a sculptor of rare gifts and prodigious skill; the present writer, who was then in training as a painter, and W. M. Rossetti, who acted as secretary to the society. In 1848 none of these men, except Collinson and Woolner, was more than twenty-one years of age. Naturally enough, Brown was solicited to become a Brother, but he, chiefly because of a crude principle which, for a time was adopted by the other painters, declined to join the society. This principle was to the effect that when a member had found a model whose aspect answered his ideas of what his subject required, that model should be painted exactly, and so to say, to a hair. Such a hide-bound rule was, of course, an absurdity, destructive of all art and hopeless. It is not to be supposed that enthusiasm for the right was the monopoly of the leading trio, or that during several years after the date in question, any one of the Brotherhood turned aside from his duty as a member. In course of time Collinson, having painted a a remarkable picture to which much less respect than is due has been awarded, and, being sorely tried by religious influences and a wavering will, openly seceded.[1]

Rossetti gallantly began and carried out his beautiful though tentative *Girlhood of Mary, Virgin*, which represents Mary and her mother, St. Anne, seated at an embroidery frame in a balcony and beneath a vine whose foliage extended over a lattice, through which is a view of a landscape without the chamber. In front of the group six books are piled, each inscribed with the name of a Virtue, while near the volume stands a child-angel, who is watering a tall lily. Joachim is trimming the vine, amid the leaves of which the Holy Dove is resting in a golden halo. The lily is not only the Virgin's emblem, but serves as a model for the embroidery she is supposed to be devoutly engaged upon while her mother tenderly and gravely regards her. The sonnet Rossetti printed in the catalogue of the Free Exhibition describes her as being

> "As it were
> An angel-watered lily, that near God
> Grows and is quiet."

This sentence sufficiently indicates the mystical and allusive mood of the painter in 1848, as well as illustrates the devout spirit which the companionship of Mr. Holman Hunt tended to strengthen while the counsel

---

[1] Walter Howell Deverell, a much beloved fellow-student, with artistic gifts time could surely have developed, was nominated, but not formally elected, to fill the place of Collinson. He died February 2nd, 1854, aged twenty-six. Collinson became a member of the Society of British Artists, which did not recognize Pre-Raphaelitism in any of its forms, and, being well advanced in middle life, died some years since. What Woolner was expected to do as a Brother I do not exactly know, but in Art and otherwise he lived a Knight of the Order of Sincerity, became a Royal Academician of great renown, and died October 7th, 1892. As for myself, having been stringently trained in the practice of Art, I found the experience thus won to be of great value in the profession of an Art-critic, into which "gentle craft" I gradually drifted, and so remain. In the same profession Mr. W. M. Rossetti has made a position of importance, besides that to which he holds as a *littérateur*. Ford Madox Brown, whose death occurred October 6th, 1893, left a name we all honour as that of one in the higher ranks of Art. It appears thus that of seven young men and Brothers five have attained eminent positions, four of them being pre-eminent, although for years after the society was formed no single member, whatever his position might be, escaped insult, obloquy, and wicked and malicious misrepresentation. The more conspicuous the Brother was the more outrageously was he attacked.

of that artist and Madox Brown helped materially the execution of the picture which, apart from its prodigious merits and simply as the first work of a painter whose training had been both brief and interrupted, I never cease to look upon with indescribable wonder. A little flat and gray, and rather thin in painting, it is most carefully drawn and soundly modelled, rich in good and pure colouring; and in the brooding, dreamy pathos, full of reverence and yet unconscious of "the time to come," which the Virgin's still and chaste face expresses, there is a vein of poetry, the freshest and most profound. Rossetti had no difficulty in finding models whose aspects he could delineate without scruple as fittest for his purpose; his sister Christina sat for the Virgin, his mother for St. Anne. The Child-angel was painted from a younger sister of Mr. Woolner, whose features did, perhaps, require a little modification. The artist's descriptive sonnet, above quoted, continued with the account of the Virgin's girlhood, which lasted

> "Till one dawn, at home,
> She woke in her white bed, and had no fear
> At all, yet wept till sunshine, and felt awed;
> Because the fulness of the time was come."

This passage distinctly points to the next picture of Rossetti, the supremely beautiful "*Ecce Ancilla Domini!*" for the *Ancilla* in which the artist's sister again sat, and which again illustrates the brooding, dreamy pathos of the painter's mystical mood, as well as the virginal charm of the lady who sat for its principal figure and face, a charm to which *The Girlhood of Mary, Virgin*, as well as the *Ecce Ancilla Domini!* manifestly owe much, although it was not the prompting *raison d'être* of both the works. There is an excellent reproduction of the latter in the *Portfolio* for 1888, with an illustrative note by the present writer.[1]

On that occasion it was said that this small picture on panel—it measures only twenty-eight by sixteen inches—is the one perfect outcome of the original motive of the Pre-Raphaelite Brotherhood by its representative and typical member. It is not correct, nor would

---

[1] *Mary, Virgin*, was priced at the gallery at £80, and sold, I believe, to the Marchioness of Bath for that price. It since belonged to her daughter, the Lady Louisa Feilding, who lent it, as No. 286, to the Academy in 1883. There is an amusing note on the selling of this picture in the *Art Journal*, 1884, p. 150.

Ecce Ancilla Domini!

it be just to say more of his influence on that much misrepresented company than admits his leadership in regard to the pathetic expression of a religious ideal. Each of the three distinguished painters whom the world now recognizes (at the time "*Ecce Ancilla Domini!*" was in hand James Collinson had to be reckoned with), so completely followed his own devices, that after a year or two, Rossetti was Rossetti alone, and hardly any traces of his genius are to be found except on his own canvases. Millais, at least, gave the painter some help in working out the highly spiritualised ideal, which may be described as follows. In a chamber, whose pure white sides and floor exhibit an intensity of soft morning light, the couch of Mary, itself almost entirely white, is placed close to the wall where dawn would strike its earliest rays, and with its head towards the window. A scanty blue curtain shaded the face of the sleeper; behind, attached to the wall, a lamp (such as in antique chambers was rarely extinguished, and supposed efficacious against evil spirits) is still alight, although it is broad day without, and the sun reveals the tree growing close to the opening. At the foot of the couch, Mary's embroidery frame, with a lily unfinished on the bright red cloth which was the sole piece of strong colour in the picture, bespeaks one of those domestic occupations painters have agreed to ascribe to the Maiden Mother. As the subjective incident of the work is the Annunciation, Rossetti intends us to suppose that the Virgin was aroused from sleep, if not from prayer, when the gentlest of the archangels appeared, the light of Heaven filled the room, and the words "*Ecce Ancilla Domini!*" were uttered by Mary in submission to her lot; for it is manifest that *The Girlhood of Mary, Virgin*, was intended to show her in a state of mystical pre-cognition, as became the sequence of the subjects.

How original were the views of Rossetti in respect to the treatment of this wonderfully difficult theme will appear when we remember how other masters had treated it. The Virgins Annunciate of Angelico, Memmi, Taddeo Bartoli, Fra Bartolommeo and others, were, as the *Portfolio* has already pointed out, generally handsomely clad, if not crowned and jewelled, and most of them are enthroned under arched canopies, adorned with sculptures. The Flemings and Germans went beyond this, and expended all the resources of their skill on Mary's brocade, precious stones, goldsmithery, and even the illuminations of the sumptuous breviary they bestowed upon her. Rossetti gave her no ornaments, except the gilded nimbus, which, as in other pictures, glows round her hair and was kindled as the angel spoke. She is covered from head to foot-heel by a simple robe of lawn, leaving her arms bare, and her dark auburn tresses fall on her shoulders, and, like the contour of her bust and limbs, have not the amplitude of womanhood. It suited Rossetti's views of his subject that the Virgin, who is almost girlish in her slenderness, should have but lately passed out of the adolescent state into a riper one. Fra Angelico, whose designs of the *Rosa Mystica* are the chastest and most original of all, witness the lovely *Annunciation* of St. Marco's convent and that other which Sir F. Burton has lately acquired for the National Gallery, never produced a maiden more passionless than this; her earnest and reverent eyes brood, not without knowledge of the pain to come (a point which had been made of yore), upon the meaning of Gabriel's salutation; while awestruck, but not overpowered, she shrinks against the wall, whose whiteness differentiates the candour of her raiment, and contrasts with the lustrous aureole of metallic gold which incloses the dark warmth of her tresses—the unbound condition of which has, of course, a meaning all readers recognize in relation to the Dove which, as in all early pictures of the Annunciation, descends from above, hovers towards Mary, and is indicated by the declaration of the Angelic harbinger. Nearly all the more ancient pictures of the Italian, German, and Low Country Schools, not less than cognate sculptured representations of this subject, give magnificent if not royal habiliments—sometimes even (as if the gentle Gabriel were the warlike Michael) archangelic coronets, armour, and weapons to the harbinger of Heaven when appearing to Mary. He is usually winged, and his vast pinions, glittering in gold, azure and vermilion, and *semée* with stars, reach from his superb tiara to the floor. A stupendous design by Holbein gives a Gabriel all glorious to behold, with pinions such as we seem to hear rustling; while in a voice mighty but subdued, he, robed like the Kaiser and grasping the sceptre of his Archangelhood, delivers his message to a round-eyed and plump Jungfrau very different from Rossetti's, while the fattest of doves appears between the imperial angel and the ponderous maiden. These figures indicate a motive quite other than that here in question, in which the stalwart, wingless harbinger, who is simply clad in white from radiant head to fiery feet, and holds the lily—an emblem and a sceptre in one—which it is his duty to deliver to Mary, approaches her with a calm and passionless face, which assorts with his noble, unmoved, and undemonstrative air, as he stands erect, and—unlike the Gabriels of Angelico, Memmi, Dürer, Del Sarto, Raphael, Giovanni Santi, Tintoret and Rembrandt—makes no obeisance to Mary, not yet crowned Queen of Heaven. In Tintoret's picture Gabriel rushes into the stately chamber of the Virgin as if on the wings of a whirlwind, and a host of angels follow him to witness the event. There is a second superb design of Holbein (now in the collection of Mr. Fisher of Midhurst) in which the grand angel, with a world of draperies flying in his haste, enters before the kneeling and tremulous Virgin, while his sword-like pinions are fully displayed as he grasps a long sceptre with one hand, and, with the other extended in a minatory way, speaks as in a voice of thunder.

This picture was begun and finished in the squalid Cleveland Street studio. The face of Mary was a just and true likeness of Rossetti's sister, and was painted with hardly any alteration of her features or expression. The face of Gabriel was founded on the features of a model named Maitland, the painter's brother, and Woolner—whose hair supplied the characteristic form and colour of the archangel's. The nimbus of the last is proper to Rossetti's masterpiece like the other emblematic lustres of the design, while there is special significance in the fiery feet of the Messenger of God. The idea of the Annunciation as a mystery, thus illustrated by the namesake of the Harbinger is imperfectly appreciated without recognition of the character of the fire streaming from the feet of the Messenger of Peace as he approached the earth.

While—not without struggles and efforts innumerable and gallant, for Rossetti's technique was, in 1849, in a somewhat uncertain and tentative condition—this picture was in progress, the *Germ* was concocted and put forth. The first number of that amazing publication appeared on "Magazine Day" of December, 1849. The last number (4) was issued soon after he wrote on " *Ecce Ancilla Domini!* " the date, March, 1850. In this year the picture was No. 225 in the Portland

Gallery, 316 Regent Street, to which place the tenants of the Hyde Park Gallery had removed their exhibition. "*Ecce Ancilla Domini!*" was priced in the catalogue at £50. It was returned unsold and remained on the painter's easel till January 1853, when Mr. McCracken, a packing agent of Belfast, who, Mr. W. Rossetti tells us, had never seen the picture, bought it for the original price; after his death it changed hands more than once, including those of Mr. Heugh, with whose collection it was in 1874 sold; for £388 10*s.* it passed to the collection of Mr. William Graham, who soon after Rossetti's death lent it to the Academy Winter Exhibition of 1883; at his sale in 1886 it was bought (price £840) for the National Gallery out of a fund bequeathed by the late Mr. John Lucas Walker. It is now No. 1210 in the Gallery.[1] It has been etched not quite successfully by M. Gaujean.

Simultaneously with the execution of *The Girlhood of Mary, Virgin*, and in the same dismal Cleveland Street studio above described, Mr. Holman Hunt painted his tentative *Death of Rienzi's Brother*, which only concerns us here because, in the rather grotesque (a term I use not depreciatingly) face of Rienzi vowing to be revenged on the boy's murderers, we have that which is by much the truest portrait of D. G. Rossetti as he appeared at that time. The pallor of his carnations was exaggerated and made more adust to suit the passion of the incident; but the large, dark eyes, strongly marked dark eyebrows, bold, dome-like forehead, the abundant long and curling hair falling on each side of the face, and especially the full red lips conspicuous in the picture are, or rather were, of Rossetti to the life. This laborious and remarkable painting having deteriorated in a deplorable manner, has been so much retouched as to have parted with nine-tenths of its historical and artistic value. About the time it was completed Madox Brown executed a much less startling version of Rossetti's head in

[1] Here is Rossetti's opinion of his own work as communicated to Mr. W. Bell Scott in a letter dated "Kelmscott, June 17th, 1874. My dear Scotus,—A little early thing of my own, *Annunciation* [this title the painter preferred for his picture when he sold it to Mr. McCracken], painted when I was twenty-one—sold to Agnew at Christie's the other day (to my vast surprise) for nearly £400. Graham has since bought it of Agnew, and has sent it to me for possible revision, but it is best left alone, except just for a touch or two. Indeed my impression on seeing it was that I couldn't do quite so well now!"

his picture of *Chaucer reading the Legend of Custance to Edward III.*, and to the present writer described his doing so in a letter[1] dated November 21st, 1882.

The latter part of the year 1849 was not only signalised in the manner above stated, but by the inception of and preparation for the publication of the *Germ*. With W. M. Rossetti for the editor the first number comprised of Dante Rossetti's writing "Songs of Our Household, No. 1," a poem, and the first version of "Hand and Soul," a prose romance in which it is impossible to avoid recognising the *quasi-*nuptial and deeply devout motives of *The Girlhood of Mary, Virgin*, and "*Ecce Ancilla Domini!*" as they clothed themselves anew in words. They are both the prototypes of those legions of poems and novelettes of which the prose and verse romances of Mr. William Morris are the most fortunate examples.[2]

[1] Here is part of the letter in question: "The *Chaucer* was exhibited at the Royal Academy in 1850 [No. 380, 1851]; at Liverpool, where it won the £50 prize, in 1859; at my own exhibition [in 1865, in Pall Mall], and bought for the public gallery at Sydney, N.S.W., in 1875. When at Liverpool it belonged to David Thomas White, who wished to cut it up (!); so I got it back from him in exchange for smaller work. Deverell, as you rightly remember, sat for the page [sitting in front, an admirable likeness of our friend]; W. M. Rossetti, who then had his hair [*i.e.* previous to his becoming bald], for the troubadour; John Marshall, the great surgeon, very kindly sat for the jester—I remember his mother's and sister's surprise! D. G. Rossetti sat for Chaucer himself, and was the very image of Occleve's little portrait. I began the head of Chaucer (Rossetti and I both at the top of a high scaffolding [in a large studio at No. 17 Newman Street, where Rossetti worked under Brown, as before stated], he reading to me), at 11 P.M., and finished it by 4 next morning; when daylight came it looked all right, so I never touched it again."

[2] *The Oxford and Cambridge Magazine*, a sort of reflection of the *Germ*, published a few years later, abounds in proofs of Rossetti's influence on Messrs. Morris and his *entourage*. The first number of the *Germ* contained, besides the above, in "The Seasons," a lovely lyric by Mr. Coventry Patmore; Miss Christina Rossetti's versed dirge, called "Dream Land," as well as "An End" by the same; a sonnet and a review by her younger brother; a delightfully fresh "Sketch from Nature," by John L. Tupper, and Woolner's "My Beautiful Lady." In "Hand and Soul" it is easy for his intimates to recognise the outpourings, protests, and introspective lamentations, the doubts, self-fears, and partial despair of his future of the author, then struggling with himself to attain means and powers sufficient for his devotion, his hopes, and his ambition. In No. 2 of the *Germ* we find the first version of "The Blessed Damozel," a poem which in after years supplied a theme and subject for one of Rossetti's most important pictures. In No. 3 he contributed "The Carillon," one of the fruits of a journey to Paris and the

It is time to set forth the prodigious influence exercised in 1847 and later by the then hardly recognized poetry of Robert Browning upon Rossetti and the more imaginative members of that circle of which he had already become the leader. This could not be better illustrated than

The Laboratory.

by the cut which, thanks to the courtesy of Mr. Fairfax Murray, is now before us and entitled *The Laboratory*,[1] of which the story is that a

Low Countries, and "From the Cliffs," a poem. In No. 4 his contributions were "Pax Vobis," and "Six Sonnets for Pictures" in the Louvre and Luxembourg at Paris, and in the Academy at Bruges.

[1] The subject for this work Rossetti found while reading at the British Museum, which, among other results, led to his introducing himself to the author of *Paracelsus* and *Sordello*, by means of a letter inquiring about *Pauline*, and expressing the highest admiration and keenest appreciation for that poet's works, then collected under the title of *Bells and Pomegranates*. "The Laboratory" originally appeared in *Hood's Magazine* in 1844, and was reprinted in No. VII. of *Bells and Pomegranates*, 1845, where, no doubt, Rossetti first

Court-lady of the *ancien régime*, who had been jilted, and become maddened by love and furiously jealous of a fairer rival, visited in his "devil's smithy" a lean old chemist and poison-monger like the apothecary in *Romeo and Juliet*, and by the gift of all her jewels, nay, the kisses of her mouth, bribed that gaunt villain to concoct a "drop."

When he had finished the dire compound, she cried to him as in the picture

> "Is it done? Take my mask off! Nay, be not morose,
> It kills her, and this prevents seeing it close:
> The delicate droplet, my whole fortune's fee—
> If it hurts her; beside, can it ever hurt me?"

The original of this cut is noteworthy as the first of Rossetti's completed works in water-colours, materials which he had not, except tentatively, till then employed, and because it has such a bold and original design, and is painted in such brilliant and strong colours that no one can regard it without surprise. Apart from the voluptuous suggestiveness—which was quite new from Rossetti—of the design, the snake-like virulence of the lady's face, the deadly passion of her clenched hand, the eager wrath of her sudden uprising, the lovely brilliance of her carnations—a little paled by rage and envy, the sumptuousness of her bust, and the vivid coloration of this striking little work attest the development of the artist in a way his biographers have failed to observe, although these

met with it and numerous other pieces which he and all his company took the highest delight in reading, and in assimilating to their hearts' content the "scraps of thund'rous epic lilted out" by the painter-poet. It was with regard to poems of Browning's that, at the time in view here, Rossetti chiefly exercised his prodigious power of reading aloud and the gigantic resources of his memory. Nearly all the P.-R.B., except perhaps Collinson, were sympathetic adepts in reading aloud, but none of them approached Rossetti, whose musical, modulated, and sonorous voice still rings in the ears of those who remember with what vigour, spirit, and poetic appreciation the comrade of those days took his part in reading thus. As to his memory of poems, that seemed inexhaustible, when nothing was missed in the recital of a *Lay of Ancient Rome*, a longish poem of Tennyson, sections of Henry Taylor's *Philip van Artevelde*, sequences of a dozen pages each from *Paracelsus* or *Sordello*, passages of Dante and other Italians faultlessly quoted, and other poetic jewellery borrowed from Leigh Hunt, Landor, Wordsworth, Chaucer, and Spenser, and stored in the mind of the poet who recited them, and was destined to add to English verse such treasures as *Sister Helen*, *Jenny*, and *The Burthen of Nineveh*. All his life Rossetti was great in reading and reciting aloud, and continued the practices to the last.

elements are noteworthy in the highest degree. They mark the opening of his second period, they excel in movement as in ardour of all kinds, remind us of Madox Brown, his true master, and, as it appears to me, owe much to what the designer had learnt during a visit made in the autumn of 1849 to Paris and the Low Countries, part of the outcome of which were the sonnets published in the *Germ* of 1850, that with rare poetic force and skill commented on several masterpieces of old art which Rossetti had studied in the Louvre and at Bruges.[1]

Pages Quarrelling.

The Laboratory distinctly reflects the intense illumination and pure colour of Memlinc's and Giorgione's (so-called) pictures at those places, to which the painter had addressed the sonnets of 1849. In the early part of the next year, he, by way of continuing his share in the *Germ*, wrote a tale of unhappy love intended for the fifth, or April number thereof, but which never appeared, although Millais etched his first plate to illustrate Rossetti's text with the design of a lady dying while sitting for her portrait. Neither the tale, which was called *St. Agnes of Intercession*, nor the etching was finished, and the latter is now one of the

---

[1] Although it is in many respects the most important of Rossetti's illustrations to Browning, *The Laboratory* is not the first of them. Previous to this he had begun in pen and ink a very elaborate and characteristic illustration to *Pippa Passes*, in three compartments, the central one of which, representing "*Hist!*" *said Kate the Queen*, seems to have gone astray. The part particularized was the original of a water-colour drawing lent by Mrs. Spring Rice, as No. 12, to the Burlington Club in 1883, and of a portion of an unfinished picture in oil, called *The Two Mothers*, which Mr. Hutton lent to the same exhibition. About 1852 Rossetti drew in ink, and gave as a keepsake to the present writer, *Taurello's first Sight of Fortune*, Burlington Club, No. 21, where it was wrongly dated "C. 1848." This work derives from *Sordello*, and is the sole illustration to that poem; it was designed to commemorate the giver's and the receiver's ardent studies anent "Sordello's delicate spirit all unstrung."

scarcest of its kind. Rossetti, too, began an etching to illustrate his own narrative, but it was soon put aside. It was about this time, or a little later, that, wanting to improve his knowledge of perspective, a subject of the Royal Academy curriculum to which he had never addressed himself, he came to me to be helped in that respect. That he was a perfectly intelligent, but not a very diligent learner is shown by the rough sketch of two medieval pages quarrelling here reproduced from among a score of such remaining on sheets of his exercises in the little science. Assuming the airs of a teacher, I had complained that he neglected his work. His reply was this sketch, intended to show what I should incur by continuing to grumble. The oblique lines athwart the feet of the figures are parts of the diagram.[1]

D. G. Rossetti.

Still later, but of the same period, is the profile portrait of himself, drawn with a pen, and here reduced from a sketch which Rossetti gave to our friend Arthur Hughes, whose picture of *April Love* is one

[1] Rossetti had so much humour that he cared little who, if good-naturedly, caricatured him, and he often sketched himself in odd circumstances and conditions. One of these sketches, made in 1849, lies before me now, and is ludicrously like in all its exaggerations of a huge head clothed by masses of dark, unkempt, curling hair, and inclosing gaunt features, a short beard and moustache, large, hollow and "detached"-looking eyes; the head is set upon sloping shoulders rounded by a slight habitual stoop, and carried forward in an eager sort of way, which is true to the life; the chest is narrow, the hips are wide. The artist's attire is the above-mentioned long-tailed dress coat, a loose dress waistcoat, and loose trousers. The sketch attests Rossetti's manner of gripping with his half-clenched fingers the cuff of his coat—a spasmodic habit which was highly characteristic of his nervous, self-concentrated temperament. Much the best description of Rossetti at this period is Mr. Holman Hunt's account of himself and "The Pre-Raphaelite Brotherhood," printed in the *Contemporary Review*, vol. xlix., p. 737; the best portrait of him, apart from the

of the most tender-hearted and subtle love-poems in the world, an idyl of ineffable pathos and sweetness.

In 1850 Rossetti completed the famous drawing in ink with a pen, entitled *Hesterna Rosa*, which illustrates the song, pregnant of sorrow and shame, of Elena, the mistress of Philip van Artevelde, in Sir Henry Taylor's noble drama. The motto of *Hesterna Rosa* is:—

> "Quoth tongue of neither maid nor wife
> To heart of neither wife nor maid,
> 'Lead we not here a jolly life
> Betwixt the shine and shade?'
>
> "Quoth heart of neither maid nor wife
> To tongue of neither wife nor maid,
> 'Thou wag'st, but I am worn with strife,
> And feel like flowers that fade!'"

The scene is a tent pitched in a pleasaunce and, though a pallid dawn gathers force among the trees, still lit by lamps from within, so that the gaunt and ghostlike shadows of a party of revellers seated in front of the design flicker and start ominously upon the canvas walls. One gambler is seated on a couch and throwing dice upon a stool placed before the group, while his companion kneels opposite and, with a goat-like action, draws between his lips the finger of his mistress, the singer, and *Hesterna Rosa* of the design, who, half hiding her face with her disengaged hand, sits behind him. He is waiting the cast of his companion's dice and will, in turn, throw his own dice upon the stool. Another girl, the mistress of the former, sits above him on the couch, and while she seems to be chanting a merry, perhaps ribald, song, has thrown her bare and beautiful arms about his neck. Near them, on our left, is a young girl holding to her ear, as if to catch the lowest throbbing of its notes, a sort of lute, while on the other side is a huge ape, grossly scratching himself, and thus intended to repeat the sensual half of the *motif* of the design, just as the lute-player repeats the sadder, less degraded pathos of the other half.

already-mentioned and somewhat exaggerated head of Rienzi, is that of the guest, who in Millais' *Lorenzo and Isabella* is drinking; here the pallor of the face is overdone, but the likeness is otherwise perfect. Mr. W. M. Rossetti sat for Lorenzo in this picture. D. G. Rossetti sat to Brown for the Fool in *Lear and Cordelia*.

CHAPTER II

1851—1861

BEFORE 1851 we find Rossetti removed to a studio on the first floor at No. 72, Newman Street, and in his art likewise removed from those hide-binding influences which inexperience forced upon him in Cleveland Street. The *Germ* having changed its name with the third number to *Art and Poetry*, had come to an end, and with it the central point, so to say, of our subject's life had shifted from the religious and mystical purposes of his first period to those intensely dramatic and romantic, and sometimes voluptuous, impulses which *The Laboratory* heralded and illustrated. The last-named year produced, besides smaller examples of less account, a fine and masculine drawing in ink, now the property of Mr. Coventry Patmore and called *The Parable of Love*, where a lady sits at an easel painting her own portrait, while her lover, stooping over her, guides her hand with his own. The motives and style of this example, which has never been engraved or copied, have even more fibre than those of *The Laboratory*. The lover is a portrait of Woolner. To be grouped with it is Mr. Boyce's brilliant and powerful drawing in water colours, called *Borgia*, for which the design in ink dates in 1850. This little piece measures only $9\frac{1}{2} \times 10$ inches, but it has that largeness of style we appreciate highly in an old master, and a brilliant and powerful coloration as well as vivid and finely harmonised colours proper, especially a rich amber and a strong black, which latter is thus, for the first time, found in Rossetti's work, and a potent element in the well conceived chiaroscuro of the whole. Lucrezia Borgia is seated on a couch playing on a lute to the sound of which a boy and a girl are dancing with wonderful spirit and energy; behind the sumptuously developed and splendidly clad dame sit the infamous Pope Alexander VI. and her brother Cæsar. The latter is blowing the rose-petals from amid the labyrinth of his sister's hair.

gazing eagerly at her, and with his dagger beating time to the music upon a half-filled wineglass at his side. Belonging to the same group as *Borgia*, and the property of the same distinguished water-colour painter and friend of Rossetti, is the original drawing in ink with a pen, styled *How they Met Themselves*, an impressive illustration of the ancient German legends anent the *Döppelgänger*, which is here reproduced from one of the two water-colour versions, painted in 1864. It is now in the possession of Mr. Pepys Cockerell, and was developed from the original.

Two lovers are walking in a twilight wood when they are suddenly confronted by their own apparitions portending death; she sinking to the earth, stretches out her arms as if appealing for mercy, while he, bolder but overawed, lays his hand upon his sword. Dramatic as it is, this design is not so virile and pathetic as the original drawing. *Giotto Painting the Portrait of Dante* is the most vigorous and apt example of 1852, and with an extraordinary sense of style and largeness in design represents the great Florentine master whom (because of the majestic simplicity of his motives and compositions) of all the old painters Rossetti most affected, sitting on a scaffold erected before a wall in the Bargello at Florence and in the act of painting that likeness of Dante, which, having been discovered by Mr. Kirkup in 1839, is still visible there. The austere poet is placed in a chair, with his knees crossed; he holds a pomegranate and maintains a dreamy, self-absorbed expression; Cimabue stands near Giotto and looks at his fellow painter's work; Guido Cavalcanti is behind his fellow poet; below, upon the pavement of the chapel, we see Beatrice in a procession of worshippers. This picture is in water colours and has all the freshness and brightness, with some of the dryness, of a fresco. The text of Dante's *Purgatorio*, c. xi. beginning

"Credette Cimabue nella pintura
Tener lo campo,"—

is most aptly illustrated by this noble design.[1]

[1] A sketch for it was shown, a most exceptional circumstance with regard to a Rossetti, as No. 7, in a " Winter Exhibition of Drawings and Sketches at 121 Pall Mall, 1852"; with it were his *Beatrice meeting Dante at a Marriage Feast* (196), and *A Sketch for a Portrait in Venetian Costume* (20). It appears that Rossetti's offered contributions

How they Met themselves.

It is certain that prices for Rossetti's pictures did not at this time "rule high." On the contrary we learn that in April, 1853, Mr. McCracken of Belfast, our painter's staunch admirer, gave him the sum of £35 for the masterpiece called *Dante on the Anniversary of Beatrice's Death*, of which a plate from the water colour drawing in the late Mrs. Combe's collection, recently given to the University of Oxford, is now before the reader.

The print shows the motives, design, and composition of the picture, but no reproduction in black and white can give an adequate idea of its subtlety, brilliancy, and colour. The subject was thus quoted by Rossetti himself from Dante's *Vita Nuova*, a mine of mystical, introspective and suggestive matter to which at this time the painter, more than before or since, devoted his attention with great energy.[1] His ideal mistress being dead, Dante wrote, "On that day which completed the year since my lady had been made [one] of the citizens of Eternal Life, I was sitting in a place apart, where, remembering me of her, I was drawing an angel upon certain tablets, and as I drew, I turned my eyes and saw beside me persons to whom it was fitting to do honour, and who were looking at what I did : and, according as it was told to me afterwards, they had been there a while before I perceived them. Observing whom, I rose for salutation and said, 'Another was present with me.'" In the design Dante is kneeling before a window opening above the Arno and Florence, and upon the sill of which stand bottles of pigments for painting, likewise a significant pomegranate, while, beneath the sill, lies with other things the quaint lute alluded to in the previous note upon "Hesterna Rosa." Dante—his attention being called from his task by the officious friend who introduced "certain people of importance" his visitors,—the impression of sorrowful thought still lingering in his eyes,—turns to look at the latter, who are an elderly magnate and his fair, tall and stately daughter. The father's action indicates that he would fain check the intrusive action of the busybody, while the lady, one

to a preceding exhibition of the same series, which was held in 1851 at the gallery of the Old Water-Colour Society, had been, as he said, "kicked out of the precious place in Pall Mall."

[1] Browning, too, in his "One Word More," published in *Men and Women*, 1855, ii. 229, sympathetically treated this subject.

Dante on the Anniversary of Beatrice's Death.

of her hands clasping the senior's hand, thus expresses her sympathy with the sorrow of Dante and her tender regret that he has been disturbed. Among the objects within the room are an hour-glass with its sand more than half run down, a flowering lily stem, a convex mirror (the existence of which at this time is challengeable), a votive picture of the Virgin and Child, and round the wall, a row of the heads of cherubs who, like

> "Carvèd angels, ever eager-eyed,
> Stared, where upon their heads the cornice rests,
> With hair blown back, and wings put cross-wise on their breasts."

Outside the chamber and beyond the half-withdrawn *portière* we see a closet with a brass cistern suspended over a basin for washing hands, one of those quite "impracticable" staircases which, as with his musical instruments, were the despair of the specialists, and, farther off, a serene landscape, comprising a sunlit meadow, a shadowy wood, and, overhead, that brooding, softly-glowing firmament, which, with Rossetti as with other poet-painters, attests the perfect peace of a Paradise beyond the grave. In this way the artist took us from the busy Arno, past the dim, half-lighted room where Dante sojourned with his grief, and through the narrow pass of Death, whose purifying function is indicated by the basin and its appurtenances, until, remote but bright, the pleasaunce of Eternity is discovered to be "beyond the veil," which is represented by the *portière*.

As in the picture before us, the often-mentioned Miss Elizabeth Eleanor Siddall, who afterwards became Mrs. Dante G. Rossetti, appears for the first time in the figure of the compassionate lady, a few lines concerning her may be acceptable. Some time late in 1850 Walter Deverell, going with his mother to a then renowned bonnet-maker's "establishment" in Cranbourne Street (then called an "alley"), and being dreadfully bored while the lady discussed a new purchase with the principal, happened in his boyish and restless mood to glance wearily along the counter to where, in the background of the shop, a group of assistants could be seen diligently building head-gear of the latest *mode*. Among these damsels sat one conspicuous by a rare sort of comeliness, tall, elegant, lithe, slim-waisted, not exuberant nor otherwise of the order

Rossetti afterwards affected, as in the *Venus Verticordia* and other sumptuous visions to which we shall come presently, but precisely of the type we recognize in the compassionate visitor of Dante. Her abundant hair was of a rich and brilliant coppery-gold tint, with brighter golden threads entwined, and bound about her small and well-shaped head, which nature poised in graceful ease upon a "neck like a tower," as Rossetti, borrowing the phrase from Spenser, said about that royal charm of one of the beauties his fancy had created. Her carnations, "rather pale than wan," were not without freckles Deverell at a distance did not see, but her fine skin was even-tinted and smooth, while her features were as choicely modelled as those of an Italian *cinque-cento* bronze. In a moment "our dear boy," as all his friends called Deverell, was on fire to paint this strangely found beauty as Viola in a picture of *Twelfth Night* he had in hand, and for whom the model must needs be filled with an inward and spiritual grace and modesty. For Walter to ask was to command his mother, and that lady exerted herself so successfully with the bonnet-maker, the damsel, and her father—who was a watchmaker originally from Sheffield and then settled somewhere in the Newington Butts region—that the desired sittings were granted to Deverell, who, poor fellow, dying young, never did the maiden justice, nor quite carried out his meaning in the picture. Soon after this Rossetti persuaded Miss Siddall to sit to him in turn, and thus began a close relationship, including Rossetti's falling in love with his model, their engagement in or about 1853, and his marrying her in May, 1860. Her death, in lamentable circumstances and some time after childbearing, occurred through an over-dose of laudanum, inadvertently taken to relieve the agonies of neuralgia. This pain was a symptom of that phthisis which had long threatened the life of the ill-starred Mrs. D. G. Rossetti. Here reproduced is a sketch of her, made by her husband at a later date (? c. 1859) than that to which we have arrived, and now the property of Mr. Fairfax Murray, who kindly lent the original for reproduction. Naturally, Rossetti made countless sketches and studies from his wife, and not seldom included her in his pictures, as in *Regina Cordium*, 1861. Several of these examples were at the Burlington Club, 1883; many more at the Rossetti sale at Christie's, May 12, 1883.

One of the most interesting pictures produced, or rather left incomplete, by Rossetti is that to which the progress of time and this narrative brings us with the year 1853. It is a work anent which, more than any other by our master, numerous erroneous statements have been made, and yet, *Found*, of the original pen drawing in ink of which, thanks to Mr. Fairfax Murray, the reader has a capital reproduction, is a noteworthy instance of Rossetti having for the nonce departed out of his then accustomed pietistic and romantic moods and entered upon a moral and modern application of design.

The Artist's Wife.

It was an entirely original work, and, in the touching, simple and veracious nature of its theme, far superior to Mr. Holman Hunt's somewhat analogous production, *The Awakening Conscience*, which, of course, preceded it before the public. It is difficult to avoid thinking that the moving and terrible story of the latter work had much to do with turning the artist's attention to, and insuring his sympathy for unhappy women of the class with the fate of whom both these pictures are concerned. Mr. Hunt must have seen it, and could not but be deeply touched. The theme, as well as the intensely realistic treatment of *Found* are completely "Huntean" and remote from Rossetti's mood, which was rather overscornful of didactic art, and thoroughly indisposed towards attempts to ameliorate anybody's condition by means of pictures.

The incident Rossetti imagined preceded, as it were, in a natural sequence that of Mr. Hunt's production. The latter implied a seduced woman in the house of her seducer; the former shows her deserted, expelled, and, whether self-wrecked or not, a wanderer in the streets of London, while we may suppose the grim Nemesis of her sex was leading her towards a veritable Bridge of Sighs, where it was but too likely the fate of Hood's

> "One more unfortunate,
> Even God's providence
> Seeming estranged,"

awaited her. The time was soon after the chilly silvery dawn had dispersed the gloom which concealed the victim, and there was light enough to reveal her form to the young countryman, who, driving townwards to market, no sooner saw the still fair face set in pale golden hair than he recognized the once pure maiden, formerly his betrothed, who, years before, had left his village and was lost in London. Leaping from the cart he seized the girl's hands and held her firmly, while shrinking to the ground, she struggled and turned her face away in vain. Beyond this the design tells its own story and we may leave it so, adding, however, that it illustrates the motto "I remember thee; the kindness of thy youth, the love of thy betrothal," *Jerem.* ii. 2, with which it is inscribed. Rossetti's original idea is expressed in the drawing now before us and some time in 1854 he, having made studies for parts of it, seems to have begun, or intended to begin, the work on the canvas. Several of the studies, squared for transferring, were included in the painter's sale. He did not get very far with the picture, the stringency of naturalistic painting not suiting his mood nor his experience. It was taken up at intervals of years, was commissioned by Mr. Leathart of Gateshead, but, not advancing, never reached that gentleman's hands; was revived in 1870, again in 1880, and commissioned again by Mr. W. Graham. As it happened, although part of the background was, after Rossetti's death, put in by another hand, *Found* was never finished as the painter meant it should have been. Despite some disproportions, questionable perspective and inequalities of details, it remains a masterpiece of poetry with exquisite parts. It is hardly needful to point out to those who have observed the allusive wealth of incidents in *Dante on the Anniversary of Beatrice's Death*, that *Found* abounds in similar details. Among these are that the girl crouches against the wall of a churchyard—"where the wicked cease from troubling, and the weary are at rest"; that the brightening dawn symbolizes, as it may be, peace (with forgiveness) on earth, or in

Found.

Heaven, after sorrow; while the calf trammelled in the net, and, helpless, carried in the cart to its death, points to the past and present life of the girl. This allusion is the least happy of Rossetti's "moralities," because, unlike the harmless beast, the woman had betrayed every one—father, mother, brother, and even the lover who had trusted her.[1]

Rossetti, who was in fairly good health at the time in question, and depressed rather than permanently defeated by the fate of *Found*, now for a while continued to design and paint in water colours, inventing his own subjects entirely, or, when older themes were adopted, giving them the new life and light of the genius which informed them with fresh fire, and left little but the title which was not his own. These themes were mostly romantic and dashed with mysticism, and they frequently referred to legends of the Arthurian cycle, the too-often dry bones and rickety whimsicalities of which Rossetti never failed to vivify, while he glorified them with light and colour. Apart from them,—and yet not quite distinct from the romantic class proper as to their poetic motives and technical treatment,—is a fine series derived from Dante, which occupied Rossetti during 1854 and 1855. Of this number the triptych of *Paolo and Francesca*, which Mr. Ruskin coveted intensely and bought, is to be reckoned. As it resembles a later version of the same subject, dated 1862, and introduced in this text, it is expedient to pass on to *The Passover in the Holy Family*, now at Oxford, the gift of the author of *Modern Painters*, which represents the porch of the house

---

[1] It is believed that the difficulties attending the completion of *Found* in the oil medium (with which he was then temporarily less accustomed to deal), and the sharp disappointment attending those difficulties, had a good deal to do with the changes of his mood and that "detachedness" which grew upon him from this time. Engaged to marry Miss Siddall, and deeply in love with her, he could not but suffer while her health was frequently broken. When the time for their wedding approached, in May, 1860, Rossetti caused the wall between Nos. 14 and 13 in Chatham Place to be broken through, and thenceforth he occupied, as in a modern flat, the second-floors in both houses. There, in February, 1862, after a very brief period of wedded union, his wife died, after which he remained no longer than, with an interval of lodging in Lincoln's Inn Fields, sufficed to secure the mansion called Tudor House, No. 16, Cheyne Walk, Chelsea, where he settled in October, 1862, and where all his later pictures that were painted in London were executed, and of which he remained the tenant till his death. It may be added that one of the best likenesses of Miss Siddall is the face of Sylvia in Mr. Holman Hunt's *Valentine Rescuing Sylvia*, painted in 1850–51.

of Joseph, as Rossetti conceived it, with Zacharias sprinkling the doorposts with symbolical blood held in a bowl by the boy Jesus, while, stooping at the feet of the latter, St. John is, notwithstanding his own declaration, fastening the shoe-latchet of the Saviour. "And Mary culls the bitter herbs ordained." Although never quite finished, this is a very pure, delicate and brilliant piece, with motives at once reverent and tender, and as Mr. Ruskin noticed, exceptionally realistic in treatment. Probably efforts made with regard to *Found* had influenced the artist to follow nature in this respect. There appears (the accounts are very confusing) to be more than one version of this example; the subject Rossetti described in one of his "Sonnets for Pictures," *Poems*, 1870, p. 266. The design, combining mysticism with types prophetic, is truly in the artist's characteristic vein. After this came the very different *Lancelot and Guinevere at the Tomb of Arthur*, a brilliant study of sunlight in an apple orchard, where, under the fruit-laden trees (here introduced significantly), lies the altar-tomb of King Arthur, with his effigies all in armour lying upon it, while the queen, habited as a nun of Glastonbury, and her quondam lover, clad in helmet and mail, have met and hold discourse about their former lives and sins.[1]

It was in 1856 Rossetti made five designs to illustrate *Poems by Alfred Tennyson*, which Moxon and Co. published in the following year, an event that, for the first time, really introduced our painter to the public at large. They are works of very great beauty, merit, and spirit, and represent *Lancelot looking on the dead Lady of Shalott, Mariana in the South, The Palace of Art* (two examples), and *Sir Galahad*. Their style, not less than their treatment, is thoroughly original, picturesque, and masculine, and quite different from any of the other illustrations in the volume.[2] Their history is well told in his brother's book. Some, if not

---

[1] Mr. W. Morris's fiery-hearted poem, *King Arthur's Tomb*, included with *The Defence of Guinevere*, 1858, illustrates the subject Rossetti chose for his drawing, and owed existence to it. While the catalogues refer to the *Morte Arthur* as the authority for the subject, I have not, although the first to describe the incident to Rossetti, been able to find anything about it in that wilderness of romance.

[2] Being drawn on the blocks direct, the original designs were unfortunately, photography not then being applied to save them, cut away by the engraver. Photographs of these originals, showing how much had been lost in the cutting, were, happily, taken from the blocks in their pristine condition. Such photographs were included in a limited

all these examples, Rossetti repeated in water-colours, and thus doubly extended his now growing reputation. *The Blue Closet*, a water-colour drawing executed for Mr. W. Morris, and now in the possession of Mr. George Rae of Birkenhead, belongs to 1857, and is one of the most romantic and, of its kind, subtlest of the artist's "inventions," which, in the justest and strictest sense of the term, it is. It is hardly necessary to say that the poet-painter had already made the colours of his pictures harmonize with their pathos, this he did even when designing the coloration of *Ecce Ancilla Domini !* in varieties of virginal white, giving the Venetian voluptuousness of Mr. Boyce's *Borgia* in sensuous splendours of diversely repeated reds, blacks, and yellows, and in the presageful gloom and terror of *How they Met themselves*, all haggard and woebegone, in the darkness of the shadow-haunted wood, and in the colours of the lover's dresses. Such harmony of subject and treatment is manifest in Mr. Rae's *Blue Closet*, an exercise intended to symbolize the association of colour with music. Four damsels appear in the composition, two of whom sing Their dresses are respectively subdued purple and black, and pure emerald green and white. They occupy the rear of the group. The other pair are instrumentalists, and play on a double-keyed clavichord (a sort of a dulcimer) placed between them, while the one pinches the strings of a lute at her side, and her companion pulls the string of a little bell hanging

exhibition of Pre-Raphaelite works which was formed in 1857 at the then No. 4, Russell Place, Fitzroy Square (now incorporated with Charlotte Street). This exhibition had of Rossetti's works, besides the five photographs, *Dante's Dream of the Death of Beatrice*, an early version of the great picture now at Liverpool ; *The Anniversary of the Death of Beatrice*, of which a plate is before the reader of this text ; an unnamed example, *Mary Nazarene ; Mary Magdalene*, *i.e.*, Mr. Ruskin's drawing ; *The Blue Closet*, Mr. Rae's beautiful picture, soon to be described in these pages, and *Hesterna Rosa*. The exhibition continued for a short time only, and had nothing to do with that of the original Hogarth Club, of 178, Piccadilly, and later, 6, Waterloo Place, which was not formed till June, 1858, when a similar exhibition to the above was set up. These designs for woodcuts were not the first of Rossetti's making ; that distinction belongs to a charming illustration of Mr. Allingham's "Maids of Elfin Mere," published with *The Music Master*, 1855, and very much injured in the cutting. It represents three damsels clothed in white, who came

> "With their spindles every night ;
> Two and one, and three fair maidens,
> Spinning to a pulsing cadence,
> Singing songs of Elfen-mere."

next to the lute. The chief colours of the foreground and its figures are those of the black-and-gold tapestry over the clavichord, the gold of the musical instruments, the white and crimson of the lute-player's garments, the scarlet, green, and white of those of her companion. As to the association of colour with music—of which this drawing is a subtle instance, more recondite than any of those examples where several old masters, and especially Rossetti himself, had made the coloration of their pictures subserve the pathetic expressiveness of their subjects—we may notice that the sharp accents of the scarlet and green seem to go with the sound of the bell; the softer crimson, purple, and white accord with the throbbing notes of the lute and the clavichord, while the dulcet, flute-like voices of the girls appear to agree with those azure tiles on the walls and floor which gave to this fascinating drawing its name of *The Blue Closet*. *The Wedding of St. George*, another design in water-colours, likewise belonging to Mr. Rae, gives play of colour with sharp notes of red, yellow, and blue in contrast, and thus suggests the clashing of the joy-bells hanging in the background, which are struck with hammers by two very quaint attendant angels. The lovers are embracing after the combat which has delivered the lady from the clutches of the dragon. St. George's gilded corselet glows under his surcoat of scarlet, and the Princess's black tresses stream past her ardent face as she nestles to his breast. The champion's brooding looks (he was probably painted from Mr. W. Morris) indicate the danger he has undergone; while the green and scaly head of the dragon, with red eyes of wrathful bloodthirstiness, is, as Rossetti was wont to say, conveniently packed in a case for despatch to Cappadocia.

The next illustration of our narrative finds a place here. It represents the prison scene in *Faust*, when the hero of Goethe's drama goes to the cell where, waiting an ignominious death because she had murdered her infant, Margaret is confined. By the aid of Mephistopheles he had provided means for her escape, but she, maddened by terror and love, passionately embraces him, and neglects his entreaties that she would seize the opportunity for flight. At the last moment the Tempter appears, as in the design, and vainly urges that it will soon be too late, and the executioners will arrive. The drawing has been kindly lent by Mr. Arthur Hughes, to whom Rossetti gave it long ago.

The Damsel of the Sangreel refers to the picture in the Union Room at Oxford, as described below, and now comes under notice. It was painted for Mr. W. Morris in 1857, and now belongs to Mr. Rae, to whom we owe much for leave to reproduce a characteristic work of the period in question, when Rossetti was deeply interested in the *Mort Arthur*,

Margaret and Faust.

of which, apart from Mr. Morris's passion for that romance, the nebulous splendours and fervours exactly suited the mood of the painter. The drawing shows a full-length figure of a damsel with dreamy eyes and com-

The San Grael.

posed lips, standing erect and still, and as if aloof from the world, her tresses spreading wide upon her shoulders, while she holds in one hand the sacramental cup, that very chalice of the raptures of Sir Galahad and his comrades of the Round Table, implying the

"Blessed Vision, Blood of God!"

which the champions sought to find somewhere upon this earth. It is a "romantic" (the painter's own term), rather than a mystically inspired version of a theme which hardly lends itself to art, and it is difficult to believe that Rossetti spontaneously attempted to deal with it.

In the next three cuts the reader has transcripts of original designs, which Mr. Fairfax Murray has kindly lent, for one of the unfortunate pictures painted in 1857–8 on the walls of the Union Debating Society's Room at Oxford. Seeing that the walls were intended to be left bare, or at worst, clothed in detestable stucco, Rossetti, who had long been ambitious of distinguishing himself in mural decoration on a larger scale, offered to enrich them with pictures associated with legends of the Arthurian cycle, such as have been referred to here. His offer, some preliminary difficulties being got over, was accepted, although it was of the most extreme rashness. It was impelled by a rare enthusiasm, and, because of the artist's absolute inexperience in painting otherwise than in oil or water-colours, was exceedingly unfortunate. Neither of these *media* being admissible, Rossetti decided to adopt distemper painting, of which, however, he knew practically next to nothing, not so much as concerned the right preparation of the walls to receive the colours, nor what pigments were trustworthy, nor how the effects of damp, gaseous and otherwise vitiated air upon the paintings were to be guarded against. He procured the aid of several brilliant artists to execute parts of the work, and so sanguine were the company that they actually hoped to finish in about a month, the series of pictures comprising numerous nearly life-size figures in well-filled compositions.[1] The

---

[1] The artists whose enthusiasm Rossetti raised to the highest pitch in this matter, were Mr. E. Burne-Jones; Mr. W. Morris, of *The Earthly Paradise*; Mr. Val Prinsep; Mr. Arthur Hughes; and Mr. R. Spencer Stanhope, whose devotional pictures are well known to the world. A more brilliant company it would, out of Paradise, be difficult to select; but not even Mr. Hughes, who was the best trained of the group, knew much of distemper painting on a large scale.

efforts of six months were almost ruined before that period was complete. At the present time the decorations are not legible. Rossetti's picture, which was never finished, is not the most dilapidated of the whole; it was intended to represent *Sir Lancelot asleep before the Shrine of the San Grael.* According to the legend it happened that, because of his sinning with Queen Guinevere the ever-victorious knight was not per-

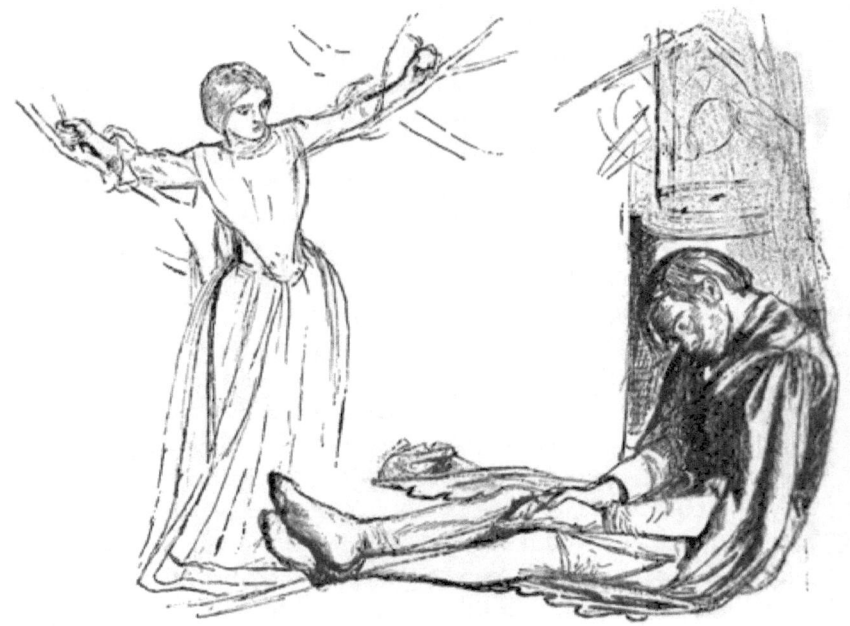

Study for Guinevere and Sir Lancelot

mitted to enter the sacred building which held the shrine: exhausted by travel and sorrow he rested on the earth outside that edifice and soon fell asleep; while in this state he dreamt that his mistress appeared to him gorgeously arrayed, and with both arms extended while she held to the branches of an apple-tree, and looked at him with queenly pride and the loving pity of an ardent mistress who beheld the sufferings of her knight. In the air behind this group the Damsel of the San Grael is seen floating, bearing the mysterious chalice that was unattainable by the impure of heart and frame, and refulgent in a sort of halo of angels. In the sketches here reproduced the reader has designs for parts of this unfortunate picture, the splendour of which, while it lasted, was at once fine

Study for Guinevere.

and intense. In one the Queen, drawn from Miss Siddall, stands with arms extended upon the branches of the apple-tree and contemplates the sleeping Lancelot, some friend or model officiating in this capacity. It is so very like the Mr. Burne-Jones of 1857, that it was certainly drawn from him. In the next design the figure of Miss Siddall, as Guinevere, appears as before holding an apple; the Damsel of the San Grael is omitted. In the third sketch we have the figure of the *Ancilla San Grael* attending the death of Sir Bors and presenting to that valiant, virtuous and holy knight the much desired chalice and the sacred bread.

Belonging to the same category as the above group of sketches, is the transcript now before us from a design for *Sir Lancelot escaping from the Chamber of Guinevere*, which is dated 1857, and was probably produced during the period of those studies in the *Mort Arthur* which bore such splendid fruit as the above instances and *The Chapel before the Lists, The Death of Breuse sans Pitié*, both belonging to Mr. Rae; Mr. Leathart's *Sir Galahad in the Chapel*, and less important works; besides two or three potent drawings concerning St. George. Of the subject of the work now before us it will be remembered that the catastrophe of the intrigue of Lancelot and his royal mistress was brought about by the foes who surprised the guilty pair. Some of Rossetti's friends have not failed to detect a satirical element in the rough sketch of *Alma Mater*, the ungirding of a knight with a sword, which, I understand, refers to the manner in which Mr. Woodward, the architect of the New Museum and the Union Room at Oxford, had been dealt with by the University authorities.

Ancilla San Grael.

Much of 1858 was devoted to the execution of Rossetti's triptych in Llandaff Cathedral, a powerful if not quite successful work which, however, need not detain us here. It represents *The Saviour adored by a Shepherd and a King; David as a Shepherd combating Goliath*, and *David as King*. In the summer of this year the Hogarth Club, of which the brothers Rossetti were important members, was founded. Among its principal objects, besides the promotion of friendly inter-

Lancelot in Guinevere's Chamber.

course, was the establishment of an exhibition room where pictures by its artistic members could be shown in a *quasi*-private manner, so that they would not be excluded from galleries, such as those of the Royal Academy, which declined works the public had previously seen.[1]

[1] This society, which must not be confused with the existing club of the same name, included some of the most eminent and accomplished artists of the day. The first meeting was held July 2nd, 1858, at 178, Piccadilly; later, the club removed to

One of the chief figures in the *Salutatio Beatricis*, which was painted in 1859, is represented by this sketch for the figures of *Dante meeting Beatrice in Eden*, half of that diptych of which the other portion illustrated *Dante meeting Beatrice in Florence*; it was painted on a door in the Red House, which, after designs by Mr. Philip Webb, Mr. Morris

Alma Mater and Mr. Woodward.

built in an orchard at Upton, Bexley Heath. This ascription is conjectural, because the sketch may refer to the *Salutatio Beatricis*, now in the possession of Mr. J. Leathart, of Gateshead. Mr. Morris has long ago parted with the Red House, and the pictures painted there by

6, Waterloo Place, Pall Mall, where it continued to meet and show pictures by its members until April 19th, 1861, when it was dissolved. Several of Rossetti's drawings were hung there.

Rossetti; mention of these suffices to recall the beginning of the latter's intimacy with the poet of *The Earthly Paradise*, which occurred some time before the *Oxford and Cambridge Magazine* was published in 1856, and was fortunate in bringing before the world the glorious *Burthen of Nineveh*, the original composition of which dates back to when, by his reading it aloud, that fine piece was made known to the author's circle of close friends. *Sister Helen*, a ballad royal if there ever was one, was likewise already known and was read in the same manner, but during the succeeding years, until 1880, or thereabouts, this poem continued to be improved. Most of Rossetti's more important pictures were, so to say, set in sonnets some of which are of priceless beauty, delightful in their colour, energy, movement and freshness. These poems, and especially the sonnets, are the outcome of a genius essentially pictorial, that is to say, a mind which saw everything—from the rose and ivory of a woman's carnations to the sullen splendour of a sunset—with the eyes of a painter revelling in colour, enraptured by the grace of a perfect curve, and capable of exquisite and sympathetic research when human pathetic expression was in view. In short, most of Rossetti's poems are pictures in words, in which respect there is a close, though partial, resemblance between his genius and that of Robert Browning.

Dante.

The next cut is of an indefinable date, probably so late as *c.* 1869, and with extreme taste and felicity, represents a graceful girl standing at a doorway and plucking apples from a tree.

Lucrezia Borgia, executed in 1860, comes next in our illustrations, and was thus, upon an unfinished and smaller version of the same, described by Rossetti himself: " *Lucrezia Borgia, Duchessa di Bisceglia.* The subject is the poisoning of her second husband, the Duke Alfonso of Bisceglia. You see him in the mirror going on crutches, and walked up and down the room by Pope Alexander IV., to settle the dose of poison well into his system." Behind those figures, as they walk in the room and are seen in the mirror, is the bed where the victim is to perish. Lucrezia, standing in front, looks calmly towards them, and, smiling to herself, deliberately washes her hands after mixing the poisoned wine and placing it in the glass vessel on the table behind her. The Pope and Duke Alfonso are supposed to be in front of the scene, and much about where we, as spectators, stand, so that she looks at them, and in her eyes there is a lurid intense light, which is horribly fine, and this illustrates what we have said as to the artist's intense research where human expression was in view. The horror of the subject is enhanced by the magnificence of the woman's form, its stateliness and its beauty. In this picture there is a great force of colour and light and shade, forming chiaroscuro of which Giorgione might boast; the whole is painted in a higher key than Rossetti had, till then, generally affected; it is solid and unusually carefully finished. Originally exhibited at the Hogarth Club, the completed version of *Lucrezia Borgia*, after remaining for a time with Mr. Leathart, passed into the collection of Mr. Rae, whose kindness allowed its reproduction for this text. About the same time, 1859-61, Rossetti began and finished the bust of a young woman, whose face, saturated with passion

Girl Plucking Fruit.

Lucrezia Borgia.

as it is, baffles description, and justifies its title of *Bocca Baciata*, or *Lips that have been Kissed*. Like the last it was first exhibited at the Hogarth Club, and, as No. 309, at the Academy's Collection of Rossetti's Works, 1883. It is in oil, very highly finished, and modelled to a pitch far above the custom of modern painters. I have long reckoned *Bocca Baciata*, although a small example, one of the finest, as it is one of the subtlest and most difficult, of pictures of our age ; it belongs to Mr. Boyce, having, moreover, that peculiar importance which attaches to the first remarkable, if not actually the first example of the artist's later, and much affected custom of painting single busts and half-length figures which, afterwards, came to be of life-size or even larger—of women, amorously, mystically, or moodily lost in dreams, or absorbed by thoughts too deep for words. In course of time a generation arose about Rossetti who knew him only by these startling, powerful and thoroughly original examples, and ignored him as a painter of *genre*, and dramatic and biblical themes.

Bocca Baciata and the Llandaff triptych being finished, or well advanced, Rossetti found time in 1860 to carry out in ink the original drawing (now the property of Mr. Boyce) of a very powerful little picture in water colours, which, in the next year, he finished at Chatham Place. This fine thing now belongs to Mr. Fairfax Murray, to whom the reader is indebted for seeing this version of the most humorous instance of Rossetti as a *genre* painter, and wit. Dr. W. Maxwell, a close crony of Johnson, told, among anecdotes of his friend, which are included in Boswell's *Johnson*, that " Two young women from Staffordshire [Lichfield acquaintances, no doubt] visited him [Johnson] when I was present, to consult him on the subject of Methodism, to which they were inclined. ' Come,' said he, ' you pretty fools, dine with Maxwell and me at the Mitre, and we will talk over that subject ; which they did, and after dinner, he took one of them on his knee and fondled her for half an hour together." Rossetti, with keen humour, has made one of the " pretty fools " a little piqued at the favour of fondling which her companion obtains, while the latter, demure, but not unmoved, sits stiffly upon the knee of the doctor, who holds forth while he stirs his tea ; Boswell, alive to the conversation, sips punch from a spoon, and the waiter, leaning over the curtain of the box, conscientiously trims the candle, and, while day sinks in the sky without, seems to wish his customers would go. Rossetti, in introducing Boswell instead of Maxwell, did so by an oversight, or more probably, because

Dr. Johnson at the Mitre.

a likeness of the former was easily obtained and sure to be recognized in his picture.

In 1861, the painter, who for a long time had had the work in hand, found himself in a position to publish *The Early Italian Poets from C.*

D'Alcamo to *Dante Alighieri*, with the *Vita Nuova* of the latter, which is the proper and almost indispensable complement to the *Divina Commedia*, a sort of autobiography of Dante in his youth and early manhood, which, as the catalogue of Rossetti's works attests, supplied him with texts for some important pictures, such as the *Salutatio Beatricis*, *Beata Beatrix*, now in the National Gallery, *Dante's Dream*, now at Liverpool, *La Donna della Finestra*, several of which we have yet to consider, and *Dante on the Anniversary of Beatrice's Death*, which has been previously described. *The Early Italian Poets* gave birth, so to say, in 1874, to *Dante and his Circle*, a nearly identical version of the former work, and did whatever a book can to extend and elevate English ideas of the poetry to which it was devoted.[1]

Rossetti's remaining works of 1861 included designs for stained glass, the logical character of which as a means of decoration, none understood so well as he.[2] A few replicas, many studies and portraits seem to have engaged the energies of our painter, while his wife's frequent illnesses, and other grave causes of distress, must have shaken him to the heart, and were more than enough to account for the fact that no serious picture proceeded from his easel until some time after his wife's death, in February, 1862, and her burial in the cemetery at Highgate. On the day of her interment he placed in her coffin, by way of sacrifice to her gentle spirit, a small volume of poems in manuscript, the greater number

---

[1] In the meantime, although Messrs. Smith and Elder published the earlier volume, the pecuniary results to the brilliant translator and learned annotator were, as his brother says, "on a very small scale." A presentation copy of the book was nevertheless priced in a bookseller's recent catalogue at £5 10s., *i.e.* about sixteen times the original sum. The volume announces *Dante at Verona, and other Poems. By D. G. Rossetti*, as "Shortly will be published," a collection which, in that form at least, never appeared.

[2] From the first he mastered the facts that, unlike pictures proper, which are seen by reflected light, paintings in glass, being transparent, are seen by transmitted light, and do not permit the use of modelling in light and shade, intended to give a false appearance of relief to that which ought to be of the nature of a mosaic in transparent media, with shadows, not modelled to anything like naturalistic or imitative results. Knowledge of this principle lies at the root of design in this application, and yet so dense was the ignorance of art then prevailing among antiquaries and *cognoscenti*, that Mr. C. Winston, a great authority as to the history of glass painting, and a first-rate copyist of ancient windows, refused to accept this rudimentary canon of the subject, and sanctioned those illogical and inartistic transparencies, which, vilely designed and childishly executed in the picture-glass works at Munich, offend the eyes of critics in

of which had been addressed to her by him, both before and during their wedded lives of less than two years' duration.[1]

St. Paul's and Glasgow cathedrals. Greatly to Rossetti's influence, though not perhaps to his initiative (about which I am not certain), is due the successful and brilliant revival of art in glass, which has flourished chiefly by means of Messrs. F. M. Brown, W. Morris, Sir E. Burne-Jones, and a few other competent artists and manufacturers, by which the whole art and practice of *vitraux* have been revolutionized.

[1] As the leading subject of this text is the art of Rossetti as it is manifest in some of the more important and characteristic of his paintings, and because it does not pretend to be a complete biography, still less, an account of him as a poet, it will be well to anticipate time, and repeat what has been often told, to the effect that while some of the poems buried in his wife's grave existed imperfectly in other versions, many, if not all of them, were complete in the small volume only. Mr. Hall Caine says that "as one by one of his friends, Mr. Morris, Mr. Swinburne, and others attained to distinctions as poets, he [Rossetti] began to hanker after poetic reputation, and to reflect with pain and regret upon the hidden fruits of his best efforts." After many searchings of the heart, as well as promptings and encouragings from friends, the poet determined to recover the volume from the grave where they had been placed as if for ever. This was done on the night of the 6th or 7th of October, 1869, and in due time the desired verses were incorporated with other examples, and issued as "*Poems, by Dante Gabriel Rossetti*, 1870." The honours of the poet were instantly acknowledged by all who had not already acknowledged them, and were worth seeking acknowledgments from. The volume, which is now scarce, contains—besides most of the sonnets already published in the *Germ*—the "Blessed Damozel," which is illustrated below, the "Burthen of Nineveh," "Dante at Verona," "Jenny," "Sister Helen," fifty supremely beautiful sonnets and songs, intended to be included in a work to be called *The House of Life* (one or more of these were afterwards withdrawn, although they reappear in the Tauchnitz edition of the *Poems*), and a body of *Sonnets for Pictures*, etc., which referred to works by the poet himself, Ingres, Giorgione, Da Vinci, Mantegna, and of Sir (then Mr.) E. B.-Jones.

I have often supposed that Rossetti might have found an authority, or example, for placing in and afterwards withdrawing his poems from the grave of his wife, in the record that when Francis I. visited Avignon, that monarch caused the tomb of Laura de Sade to be opened, and took from it a small box containing verses which had been written by Petrarch's own hand, and were placed there by him; they were afterwards, by order of the King, returned.

CHAPTER III

1861—1882

WHEN he recovered from the shock of his wife's death, which was not till some months had passed, and he was settled in the large house at Cheyne Walk, a new and energetic sphere of life opened before our painter, of which almost the first output was Mr. Leathart's triptych in water colours of *Paolo and Francesca* (R.A. 1883, No. 291), a developed version of a design which Mr. Ruskin had some years before bought, and which is very well represented here by a transcript from one of Mr. Rae's treasures (Burlington Club, 1883, No. 13).

This is altogether a sadder and more sombre work than Mr. Leathart's. The first compartment represents with extraordinary power the kissing in the garden house; the second the floating of the condemned pair in the dark regions, where in the irresistible air they roll as leaves roll in a strong current, still clasping each other, and with folded feet and garments all composed; moving both as one they pass amid the rain of sapphire-hearted flames. The third compartment, the motto of which is "*O lasso!*" the poet's cry of pity, refers to the second division, and exhibits Virgil and his disciple walking in the gloom, Dante regarding the lovers with pitying eyes, and holding his loose garment to his lips. In the first division, Paolo has looked up from the pictured page of the book the princess and he read together, and, all on fire at heart, seen answering fire in Francesca's eyes; so he clasps both her hands in both of his, and they indulge with equal passion in the luxury of love. Abandoning her lips to his, she, under levelled eyelids, gazes on his face while it meets hers.

The Bride, or *The Beloved*, a noble picture which I regard as Rossetti's masterpiece—one only example, to wit *Proserpina*, to which we shall shortly come, being in my opinion fit to be compared with it—dates its origin from 1863,[1] and as regards its splendour and colour and the passion

---

[1] A letter from the painter to Mr. Rae, dated "December 22nd, 1863," mentions that his correspondent had previously seen the *Beloved* in a not quite finished condition.

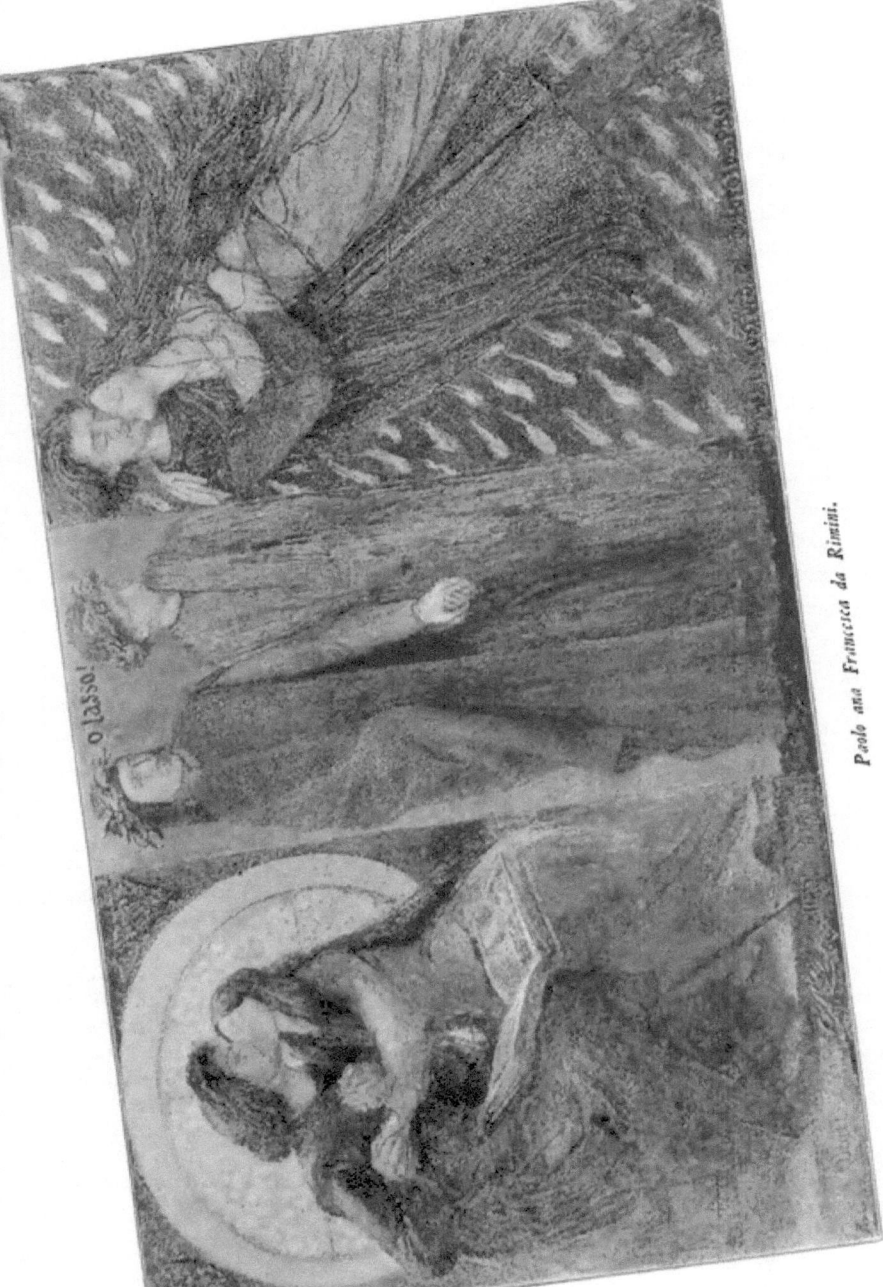

Paolo and Francesca da Rimini.

of its design, need not fear comparisons with the greatest works of the sixteenth century in Venice. In these respects this *chef d'œuvre* is a superb and ardent illustration of the Song of Solomon, "*My Beloved is mine, and I am his; let him kiss me with the kisses of his mouth for thy love is better than wine.*"

The picture comprises—as if they had halted in a marriage procession, towards the spot where the enraptured bridegroom awaits them—five life-size adult maidens and a negro girl, who, in the front of the group, and bearing a mass of roses in a golden vase, is adorned with barbaric jewellery, all of which harmonizes with her dusky skin, which, although it has the true Titianesque ruddy undertint, is of a deep bronze-brown surface hue. The negress and her burthen are intended to contrast intensely with the costume and face of the bride herself, who is clad in an apple-green robe, as lustrous as silk and as splendid as gold and embroideries of flowers and leaves in natural colours can make it. This garment and its decorations support the colour of the dark maid's skin and heighten the value of the pure red and white of the bride's carnations, while the contours of the African's face and form contrast with the Caucasian charm of the bride, her stately countenance, and "amorous-lidded eyes."

The *Song* is aptly illustrated by the attire of the bride and her companions; it says, "She shall be brought unto the king in raiment of needlework; the virgins that be her fellows shall bear her

In the February following Rossetti wrote again, and his note is an amusing illustration of that business capacity in which, as a bargain-maker, cash-receiver, and negotiator in general, he, to the wonder of his artistic and poetry-loving friends, shone greatly. Of his powers in these respects, bankers, lawyers, merchants, and everybody whose wisdom in cash and commerce was unchallengeable, spoke with unreserved admiration, not to say surprise. Mr. Leyland, who had ample experience as a buyer of Rossetti's works, humorously, kindly, and in the terms of Lowell's poem, joked about him as "a darned hard hand at a deal." A capital illustration of his ability in the managing of his affairs and negotiating the sale of his pictures is before me, in a latter to Mr. Rae, dated February 24th, 1864, proposing to sell five drawings, including *The Blue Closet* and *Paolo and Francesca*, which are before the reader, to the Liverpool banker. Of these, he wrote, "the purchaser would have to arrange with me for the completion of the unfinished drawings," which were then in Mr. W. Morris's collection. "No opportunity," he urged, "is ever likely to occur again of obtaining drawings of mine at such a price, since they are all good specimens of my work." Than these statements nothing could be truer.

company, and shall be brought unto thee." On either side of the bride appear two damsels, not yet brides. The principal figures are differently clad, diverse in face and form, and to some extent contrasted in character and expression. Besides her robe the bride wears about her head and throat a veil of tissue differing in its green from that of the robe, and above her forehead rises an aigrette of scarlet enamel and gold, that resembles in some respects the peculiar headdress of ancient Egyptian royalty ; this is set like a coronet upon her hair. While advancing towards the bridegroom, with an action at once graceful and natural, she, half thoughtfully, half in pride of supreme loveliness, has moved the tissue from her face and throat. With the same movement she has thrown backwards a large ringlet of her hair, revealing the softened dignity of her loveladen eyes, as well as her face, which is exquisitely fair and fine, and has the least hint of blushes within the skin, as though the heart of the lady quickened, while we see there is tenderness in her look, but voluptuous ardour nowhere.

All the four maids seem to have been chanting a nuptial strain, while they have moved rhythmically with the steps of the bride.

Excepting one or two later works of the master, where sentiment of a more exalted sort, as in *Proserpina*, inspired the designs, *The Beloved* appears to me to be the finest production of his genius. Of his skill, in the high artistic sense, implying the vanquishment of prodigious difficulties—difficulties the greater because of his imperfect technical education—there cannot be two just opinions as to the pre-eminence of Mr. Rae's magnificent possession. It indicates the consummation of Rossetti's powers in the highest order of modern art, and is in harmony with that poetic inspiration which is found in every one of his more ambitious pictures. This example can only be called Venetian, because of the splendid colouring which obtains in it. Tintoret produced works which assort most fortunately with this one, and his finely dramatic mode of designing reappears, so to say, in *The Beloved*, where the intensity of Venetian art is exalted, if that term be allowed, in a modern strain, while its form, coloration, and chiaroscuro are most subtly devised to produce a whole which is thoroughly harmonized and entirely self-sustained. Of how few modern instances could this be said? The colouring of this picture supports the sentiment of the design in the happiest manner, and in its magnificence the work agrees with the chastity of the conception. There is a nuptial inspiration throughout it, even in the deep red of the blush roses the negress bears. The technique is so fine that it leaves nothing to be desired, even in the lustrousness of the gold vase, in the varied brilliancy of the robe of the bride, in the subtle delicacy of the carnations, solidly and elaborately modelled as they are and varied to suit the nature of each of the figures. Rossetti's *Beloved* is in English art what Spenser's gorgeous and passionate *Epithalamium* is in English verse, and, if not more rapturous, it is more compact of sumptuous elements.

We must hasten past several capital examples, besides minor pictures and studies which occupied the easels of Rossetti at this epoch, and devote attention to *Beata Beatrix*, that poetic version of his lost wife, which is her best if not her only monument, and one of the finest examples in the National Gallery. Dream-like, and of a dream, he painted this wonderful picture, which, if the *Bride* is an epithalamium, must surely be called a nuptial dirge. In some respects it is, as I have said in *The Portfolio* of 1891, even more distinctly than that superb achievement, *The Beloved*, a full and true reflection of the artist's idiosyncrasy of the higher order. The mysticism and mystery of *Beata Beatrix* are due to that which was, so to say, the innermost Rossetti, or Rossetti of Rossetti. The Beatrix of Dante's imagination, sits in a balcony of her father's house in Florence. The picture places us in the chamber from which the balcony opens, and the damsel's form is half lost against the outer light, half merged in the inner shadows of the place. She is herself a vision while—her corporeal eyes losing power of outward speculation—the heavenly visions of the New Life are revealed to the eyes of her spirit. The open window gives a view of the Arno, its bridge, and the towers and crowded buildings of that city in which Dante and Beatrix spent their lives till the fatal month of June, 1290, when she died, and, as the poet tells us, "the whole city came to be, as it were, widowed and despoiled of all dignity," or as the frame in the National Gallery has it, as a motto, uttered when her death was announced to him, and borrowed from Jeremiah, "*Quomodo sedet sola civitas.*" In the picture the form of Beatrix is opposed to the dun evening light of the outer world, and so placed that the light shines through the outer threads of her dark auburn hair, and thus produces the effect of a saint-like halo, while the face itself, is to our

Study of a Head.

sight, merged in the dimness caused by our looking at the splendour of the river. Accordingly, the figure appears partly outlined against the lustre, partly lost in the half-gloom of the chamber. It is thus visible in what may be called a twilight of brilliance and a twilight of shadow, and the abstruseness of the design is manifest. Her form is merged, not lost, in that shadowy space which, in Butler's happy phrase, is "of brightness made." Thus Rossetti happily showed that his subject was a mystery, not without life of this world, nor all unreal.

As to the picture itself and its spectators, it is obvious that we remain on the mundane side of things, while Beatrix in a swoon passes into the Valley of the Shadow of Death, and the Florence that Rossetti painted is the Heavenly City of the Future. Her features look pale in the half gloom, and her hands, which erst clasped each other in her lap, have fallen apart to lie supine because their task is almost done, and this is celestial light that glances on them. A dove, of deep rose-coloured plumage, and, like the bird of the Annunciation, crowned with an aureole, poises on downward wings at her knees, and bears to Beatrix's hand a white poppy—*i.e.*, the mystical flower in which Rossetti meant to combine the emblems of death and chastity. Her face is in most respects a likeness of the painter's wife, but it is obvious that, although it was not intended for a portrait of the lady, it may well be called a spiritual translation, inspiring features which had but a general resemblance to those of Beatrix which he depicted with so much pathos. In the background the poet Dante attentively regards the figure of Love the ideal Eros of his vision, who, holding a flaming heart, passes on the other side of the picture heavenwards, and seems to sign to him that he should follow in that path. This vermilion-clad genius is, of course, the *Eidolon*, Spiritual Beatrix, or celestial Love, whose earthly image was the Beatrix the poet made immortal in immortal verse.[1]

We have now to pass to Mr. Rae's *Sibylla Palmifera*, the noble seated figure of a virgin, quiet and pale, as if long absorbed in the contemplation of the mysteries of life and thought, and holding a palm before a shrine,

[1] This picture was begun in 1863, finished in 1865, bought in 1866 by the Hon. W. Cowper Temple, created Lord Mount-Temple. After his death his widow, who exhibited it at the Academy in 1883, partly to carry out his wish, partly in honour of the artist, gave it to the National Gallery. There are two, not so fine, versions of it in oil, besides a repetition, if not two, in water colours, a drawing in crayons, and various studies for parts of this work. The *Portfolio*, 1891, contained an etching from this picture.

Venus Verticordia.

while at her side burns a lamp whose steadfast flame rises towards a garland of roses which hangs near the sculptured head of a cherub; on the other side is a thurible from which smoke ascends slowly in circles, towards a Death's-head, over which is suspended a wreath of poppies. Above the sibyl's head hangs a festoon of olive boughs and, carved in a niche, is a sphinx, with other emblems of mysteries. Two butterflies, one of gold, the other of a carnation tint, whose significance may be easily imagined, hover near the sibyl's shoulder. The coloration of this fine work, of which Rossetti thought very highly, is as apt and powerful as that of *The Beloved*, but, of course, of a very different kind; it expresses pathos of quite another sort, and, so to say, is such as Milton would desire for

> "Him that yon soars on golden wing,
> Guiding the fiery-wheeled throne,
> The Cherub Contemplation."

As was his wont in several cases, our painter wrote a fine sonnet illustrating this picture and its theme, and published it in *Poems*, 1871. As these lines are reprinted as "Soul's Beauty" in *Ballads and Sonnets*, the reader will be pleased to find it here. Like the picture, the sonnet has its antithesis in "Body's Beauty," or "Lilith," which is described below.

SIBYLLA PALMIFERA.

"Under the arch of life, where love and death,
   Terror and mystery, guard her shrine, I saw
   Beauty enthroned; and though her gaze struck awe,
I drew it in as simply as my breath.
Hers are the eyes which over and beneath,
   The sky and sea bend on thee,—which can draw,
   By sea or sky or woman, to one law,
The allotted bondman of her palm and wreath."

"This is that Lady Beauty, in whose praise
   Thy voice and hand shake still,—long known to thee
     By flying hair and fluttering hem,—the beat
    Following her daily of thy heart and feet,
   How passionately and irretrievably,
In what fond flight, how many ways and days!"

On *Venus Verticordia*, for leave to reproduce the water-colour version of which we are indebted to Mr. Rae, Rossetti wrote a passionate sonnet which, as it contrasts intensely with the above example, and because it describes the picture in splendid words, may be welcome here from the edition of 1870, which is repeated from the text on the frame of Mr. Rae's picture:

VENUS

"She hath the apple in her hand for thee,
    Yet almost in her heart would hold it back;
    She muses, with her eyes upon the track
Of that which in thy spirit they can see.
Haply, 'Behold, he is at peace,' saith she;
    'Alas! the apple for his lips,—the dart
    That follows its brief sweetness to his heart,—
The wandering of his feet perpetually!'

"A little space her glance is still and coy;
    But if she gives the fruit that works her spell,
Those eyes shall flame as for her Phrygian boy.
    Then shall her bird's-strained throat the woe foretell,
    And her far seas moan as a single shell,
And her grove glow with love-lit fires of Troy."

She stands before a maze of honeysuckle flowers and foliage, to obtain which Rossetti wrote to Mr. Rae that he "lost a whole week, and pounds on pounds," and it is backed by a dense mass of roses of rich varieties and depths of tone; it is as if—all fresh and blushing in the daylight—she, nearly naked, stood in a wilderness of flowers; her face is that of a woman, young, tender and ardent, but not without the wistfulness of pity which is indicated by the verses.

We are now studying the very highest examples of Rossetti's genius during its second, or third, and most sumptuous manifestation. Of the productions of the period embracing 1864 to 1872, few surpass and few approach *Lilith*, of which a transcript from a photo-

---

[1] There are two versions of this subject, more or less resembling the example before us, and painted in oil; that which (dated 1868) Mr. W. Graham lent, as No. 305, to the Academy in 1883, was originally the largest and finest of all. It was much injured by repaints, and sold in 1885 for £588.

graph, taken before certain alterations which some critics consider improvements, is now before the reader. Rossetti might have got a hint from that

Lilith.

delightful repertory of whim, wit and learning, the *Anatomy of Melancholy*, by R. Burton, who wrote " The Thalmudists say that Adam had a wife called Lillis, before he married Eve, and of her he begat nothing but devils." On this hint, and, perhaps from a few lines in Shelley's translation of *Faust*, the painter-poet set about to educe in solid form his notions of the fair and evil-hearted witch, who, as a sort of Lamia, had been originally formed like a serpent. He painted her as a modern type of the "Body's Beauty," and endeavoured, by the forces of contrast and antithesis, to make more distinct the nobler, because chaster, charms of *Sibylla Palmifera*. As with regard to the latter, so with *Lilith* he illustrated his meaning in the following sonnet.

BODY'S BEAUTY.

"Of Adam's first wife, Lilith, it is told
   (The witch he loved before the gift of Eve),
  That, ere the snake's, her sweet tongue could deceive,
And her enchanted hair was the first gold.
And still she sits, young while the earth is old,
   And, subtly by herself contemplative,
  Draws men to watch the bright net she can weave,
Till heart and body and life are in its hold.

"The rose and poppy are her flowers; for where
  Is he not found, O Lilith, whom shed scent
And soft-shed kisses and soft-shed sleep shall snare?
   Lo! as that youth's eyes burned at thine, so went
   Thy spell through him, and left his straight neck bent
And round his heart one strangling golden hair."[1]

As Rossetti painted *Lilith* she appears in the ardent languor of triumphant luxury and beauty, seated as if she lived now, and reclining back in a modern robe, if that term be taken rightly; the abundance of her pale golden hair falls about her Venus-like throat, bust and

---

[1] The sonnet written on the frame of that version of this picture which belonged to the late Mr. F. Leyland (Burlington Club, 1883, No. 47), is not quite the same as this. The original version belongs to Mr. Bancroft, junior, of Wilmington, Delaware, U.S.A. The charming actress, whose stage name was Miss Herbert, and who sat more than once to Rossetti, was not, I believe, the model for this face and form. The reader will find some curious matter about Lilith and similar fair witches in *Notes and Queries*, Sixth Series, vols. viii. and ix., under "Curiosities of Superstition in Italy," and written by Mr. R. H. Busk. A reduced version of the work before us is in water-colours, with the face altered, and is, or was, in the collection of Mr. Alexander Stevenson, of Tynemouth (B. Club, 1883, No. 55).

shoulders, and with voluptuous self-applause—an element of the design rendered with ineffable imagination and skill—she contemplates her features in the mirror her left hand holds, while with the other hand, using a comb, draws apart the long filaments of her hair. The haughty luxuriousness of the beautiful modern witch's face, the tale of a cold soul amid all its charms, does not belie, such was the art of the master in painting it, the fires of a voluptuous physique. She has passion without love, and languor without satiety—energy without heart, and beauty without tenderness or sympathy for others—for her lovers least of all. She holds the mirror with negligent grace, and, self-absorbed, trains her bewitching locks, letting them fall as her slow fingers move in their long masses. Thus occupied, she is reckless how much or how little of her bosom and shoulders is displayed in a delicious harmony of colour with the warm white of her dress, heedless of the grace of her attitude, and the superb abundance of her form. A larger mirror stands behind the lolling figure, and reflects a garden; beyond the lady a mass of roses bloom. These blossoms of strong and varied hues, the warmer ivory of her carnations, with inner rosy tints paler than the flowers, and the diverse whites of Lilith's garments, including an ample mantle lined with fur, are charming elements of a fine coloration. The expression of the witch's face is, in the water-colour version, at once more amorous and more cruel than that of the picture in oil, and I am at one with Mr. W. Rossetti in preferring the former face, which retains the painter's original intention, to the latter, which is due to revision at a latter period, although the oil version itself is still dated 1864; the reduced instance in water colours being dated 1867. Such are the delays incident to painting great pictures.[1]

Passing Mr. Craven's *Washing Hands*, a lady by that action significantly dismissing a lover (B. Club, 1883, No. 54); Mr. Rae's vigorous

---

[1] Here is part of a letter from the artist to Mr. Rae, setting forth causes of repeated delays in finishing the picture now in question :—" Feb. 1, 1866. . . I hope to have made some progress with *Palmifera* by the time the *Beloved* reaches you, but cannot expect very much. So don't be surprised, if you come soon, to see no great advance. It may be otherwise, however—there is no knowing in such a lottery as painting where all things have a chance against one—weather, stomach, temper, model, paint, patience, self-esteem. self-abhorrence, and the Devil into the bargain."

tragedy called *A Fight for a Woman*, two knights in a duel ; *The Blue Bower* (not the same as Mr. Rae's *Blue Closet*, but a half-length figure of the sitter for *Bocca Baciata* and *Lilith*), which belongs to Mr. Craven ; the charmingly fresh and pure *Il Ramoscello*, the bust of a young girl, of which, prefixed to Mr. Colvin's accomplished essay on Rossetti, there is a good woodcut in the *Magazine of Art*, 1883 ; *Regina Cordium*, a head in oil of the beautiful Miss Wilding ; we come to Mr. Rae's superb *Monna Vanna*, or *The Lady with the Fan*, which has something that is evanescent and fickle in her expression, a self-centred character revealed by every feature, lovely as these are. The ends of a long coral necklace are about her wrists, and she is drawing the carcanet slowly round her neck ; a heart-shaped jewel of clear white crystal is suspended on her breast, a hard, cold, colourless gem that is significant of her soul and its impulses : she holds a fan of brown feathers, like those of a pheasant's wing, and wears a robe of white tissue, the folds of which are at once beautiful and unstable, embroidered with gold in lines that scintillate here and there. Her lips that have been often kissed are cherry-coloured, ripe and full, yet not warmed by inner passion, nor exalted by rapture of contemplation, as those of *Sibylla Palmifera*, still less are they chaste and untasted like those of the maiden of *Il Ramoscello*. Painted in 1866, and repainted in 1873, this picture was No. 302 in the Academy, 1883. It is sometimes called *Belcolore*, but is quite different from a work of 1863 which is so named, and shows a girl biting a rosebud. A choice work in oil called *A Christmas Carol*, a young girl singing with gladness to a lute, dates from 1867, and belongs to Mr. Rae. It has been well etched by M. Gaujean. In this year we reckon *Tristram and Iseult drinking the Love-Potion*, the latest of Rossetti's illustrations of the Arthurian legends, as a very telling representation of a fine and pregnant subject. It belongs, or lately did so, to Mr. Leathart, and in some respects may be ranked with *The Loving Cup*, an inferior version of which was recently in the Leyland Collection ; Mr. Graham's of a later date is better.

No production of 1868 by Rossetti charms the student more than the noble *Aurea Catena* (now the property of Lord Battersea), sometimes called *The Lady with the Chain*, a sort of portrait of Mrs. W. Morris, which from a drawing in crayons forms the subject of our next illustra-

The Lady with the Chain.

tion, and is the first of a very numerous category of pictures, cartoons, and studies from that lady.

The design of this beautiful work explains itself, and needs no more to be said than correcting the error which has named it as *La Pia*, a title due to an oil picture of 1868, illustrating the fifth canto of the *Purgatorio* of Dante, which belonged to Mr. Leyland and, if space permitted, should have ample attention in this text.[1]

[1] There is only a general resemblance between the designs of *Aurea Catena* and *La Pia*. The unhappy lady who bore the latter name, Pia de' Tolomei, was wife of Nello della Pietra of Siena, who, until she died there, was confined by her husband in a fortress of the fever-haunted Maremma. In Rossetti's picture she is dressed in blue and white drapery, seated behind the rampart of her prison, with heart-breaking languor and despair looking over the plain and moodily trifling with her fatal wedding ring. *La Pia* was No. 319 at the Academy, 1883, and at Mr. Leyland's sale, May, 1892, sold to Mr. Bibby for 300 guineas, a comparatively small price for a Rossetti in good condition, and measuring 42 × 48 inches. It was not finished till 1881, and is therefore one of the master's latest productions. Together with the *Day Dream*, *La Pia* is described at length in the *Athenæum*, 1881, No. 2783. Dante met the unquiet spirit of Pia de' Tolomei in Purgatory, among those whose opportunity of repentance was only at the last moment, and who died without absolution. From the *Purgatorio* the artist thus translated her appeal to the Italian poet—

"'Ah! when on earth thy voice again is heard,
And thou from the long road hast rested thee,'
(After the second spirit said the third),
'Remember me who am La Pia; me
Siena, me Maremma, made, unmade,
This in his inmost heart well knoweth he
With whose fair jewel I was ringed and wed.'"

Such a theme as these lines indicate is very different from that of the picture before us, although the works make it obvious that the same lady sat for both. Before me lies an autograph version of the translation as above, which in the fifth line differs from that engraved upon the frame of the painting, being—

"From Siena sprung, and by Maremma dead."

The alteration shows Rossetti's extreme care in translating and adapting texts to his pictures, and was effected between my visit to him, when the work was available, and the engraving of the lines on the frame. As previous pages have shown it was Rossetti's frequent custom to write illustrative verses on the frames of his pictures such as this, *The Day Dream*, *Proserpine*, and the like. The practice was a survival of what he had done when writing the sonnets published in the *Germ*, and it was continued to his last days. Not all these verses are included in the published volume of the artist's poems. *Aurea Catena* was Lot 38 in the Rossetti sale catalogue at Christie's, May 12, 1883.

In its preparation, if not in its completion, following *Aurea Catena*, we find our subject dealing with *Rosa triplex*, a water-colour drawing for Mr. W. Graham, and representing three beautiful female heads, delineated alike in different views of Miss Alice Wilding, one of the loveliest models who sat to Rossetti not only for this noteworthy group, but for the heads of the ladies in *Sibylla Palmifera*, *Veronica Veronese*, *La Ghirlandata*, *The Sea Spell*, *The Roman Widow* (otherwise *Dis Manibus*) and various drawings and studies of choice qualities. She began to sit to him, I think, about 1864, and continued to do so till about ten years later, and, in regard to her form and air, he never adopted a more exquisite type of womanhood, *per se*. As a type she partially succeeded Miss Ruth Herbert, as that lady named herself in public, and in the later portion of her decade, was to some extent superseded by Mrs. Morris, who sat to the painter so often and to such marked effect that idle critics, ignorant of the facts, were accustomed to censure Rossetti for always, as they said, depicting the same type of womanhood. As to this, the truth has been set forth by the artist's brother, who enumerated not fewer than fourteen different models whom our common subject had excelled with, to say nothing of those who sat for inconsiderable heads or were not literally represented in pictures and studies of all sorts. There are not fewer than five versions of *Rosa triplex*, of the first and best of which, dated 1867, the *Portfolio* in 1892 gave a fine reproduction from the red chalk drawing in the National Gallery, a bequest of Mr. J. J. Lowndes, who died in 1891. Here is part of what the *Portfolio* published concerning the versions of *Rosa triplex*, the history of which illustrates so many of the characteristics of Rossetti and his art, that I should be sorry to omit it from these pages.

"In all these cases the artist worked, so to say, simply as a devotee of Beauty in one manifestation of that divine element, but with no distinct intention to develop the spiritual essence of his ideal by imparting to the luxurious and refined physical aspect of the person in question those mystical impressions which pervade *Sibylla Palmifera*, the romantic inspiration of *Veronica Veronese*, the spirituality which, to the heart of it, is Italian of the sixteenth century, or *La Ghirlandata's* dreamy amorousness, the spell of which she is weaving with the notes of the harp whose strings her fingers slowly and daintily caress. The rapture of her deep blue eyes attests the secret of the throbbing music which loses itself amid the foliage of her bower; so intense is the inspiration of the picture. Nor in depicting *Rosa triplex*, was Rossetti seeking to express

"'In Venus' eyes the gaze of Proserpine,'

which was the poetic motive of his *Pandora*, instinct with mysterious trouble."

So many differently inspired versions did Rossetti give us of the beauty of Alice Wilding. Nevertheless, I dare say, not a little of her charm existed mostly in the passionate heart of the painter; yet I well remember that nothing he drew of her, diverse as the delineations were, seemed less than an exact likeness. Of course, one saw her through the mood of the artist and it has sometimes appeared to me that the ardent sonnet he called *The Portrait* referred, however generally, yet chiefly, to her, when he described how, when "my lady's picture" was finished he exclaimed——

"Lo! it is done. Above the long, lithe throat
The mouth's mould testifies of voice and kiss,
The shadowed eyes remember and foresee.
Her face is made her shrine. Let all men note
That in all years (O Love, thy gift is this!)
They that would look on her must come to me."

Did ever lover, poet and painter write of his mistress more finely than thus? In *Sibylla Palmifera* the model of *Rosa triplex* is presented in an impressive light, and the artist himself appears therein characteristically as the devotee of that intellectual beauty which Shelley named

"The awful shadow of some unseen power."

Rossetti's sonnet on the sibyl I have already quoted.

La Bionda del Balcone (the blonde Lady of the Balcony) followed *Rosa triplex* in the same year, 1868, and was succeeded by *The Princess Sabra drawing the fatal Lot*, both in water colours. Then, in 1869, among other less important things, came *La Donna della Finestra* (The Lady at the Window) otherwise *The Lady of Pity*, and supposed to be that dame who, according to the *Vita Nuova*, looked with profound compassion upon Dante when he noticed her weeping because of the death of Beatrice. He was entirely lost in his sorrow, and looking up, saw a young and beautiful lady pitifully regarding him from her window. The first version of this subject Rossetti made in crayons and sold to Mr. W. Graham, it was afterwards reproduced in photography and published; next, in 1879, came, if I understand the painter's brother rightly, a version in oil which Mr. F. S. Ellis bought, and thirdly, in 1881, a somewhat different version of the same design, which the artist left unfinished, and comprising the head and hands only. A study in chalks of *The Lady of Pity* was Lot 23, at Rossetti's sale. Lot 101 in the same sale was a picture in oil, including the head and hands only, and this, doubtless, is the original of the cut before us. This, although the sale catalogue gives its date as *c.* 1878 (the date of Lot 23, being *c.* 1875), I, following a rule adopted in this text, place here, according to Mr. W. Rossetti's date of the primary type of the whole category, *i.e.*, Mr. Graham's version of *La Donna della Finestra*. Mr. F. S. Ellis's version was No. 321 in the Academy, 1883, and dated 1879.[1]

The earliest rendering of *Pandora*, which is in crayons, dates from 1869 and belonged to Mr. T. Eustace Smith, who lent it to the Burlington Club in 1883. Mr. John Graham had a version in oil (R.A. 1883, No. 320), dated 1871. It represents a half-length figure, with long, dark auburn hair, in red drapery, and holding a casket inscribed "Nositur ignoscitur," and from which a red flame issues. Rossetti wrote a sonnet for this picture, which, as it illustrates its poetical and pathetic motives, and is not reprinted in *Ballads and Sonnets* may be quoted here :—

PANDORA.

"What of the end, Pandora? Was it thine
The deed that set these fiery pinions free?
Ah! wherefore did the Olympian consistory
In its own likeness make thee half divine?

---

[1] If the reader is of a generous, not to say a merciful, disposition, he will in these and other instances forgive possible errors in dating examples mentioned in this text. The confusion of the titles, dates and descriptions of Rossetti's works remains great, although the painter's brother has done much to lay straight the threads of a tangled skein of records.

The Lady of Pity.

> Was it that Juno's brow might stand a sign
>   For ever? and the mien of Pallas be
>   A deadly thing? and that all men might see
> In Venus' eyes the gaze of Proserpine?
>
> "What of the end? These beat their wings at will
> The ill-born things, the good things turned to ill—
>   Powers of the impassioned hours prohibited.
> Aye, hug the casket now! Whither they go
> Thou mayst not dare to think, nor canst thou know
>   If Hope still pent there be alive or dead."

Neither the picture nor the sonnet is a first-rate work of Rossetti's, though they both illustrate his power of projecting himself into a subject which, in itself, seemed to have been made on purpose for him.

The next important picture by our poet-painter is that which many consider to be his *chef-d'œuvre*, to wit, the famous *Dante's Dream*, now in the Walker Art Gallery in Liverpool, where it was placed as a masterpiece. Mr. W. Rossetti has told at length the history of this very fine and impressive work, which, begun in 1869, continued to be a sort of heroic white elephant, remaining chiefly in the painter's studio till 1881. I do not intend to enter into this subject now—the picture having been again and again before the public—or to describe at length the grand and monumental design itself. Suffice it that, when at the Academy in 1883, it was thus, in the painter's own memoranda, explained: "The scene is a chamber of dreams, strewn with poppies, where Beatrice is seen lying on a couch, as if just fallen back in death; the winged figure of Love, in red drapery (the pilgrim Love of the *Vita Nuova*, wearing the scallop shell on his shoulder) leads by the hand Dante, who walks conscious but absorbed, as in sleep; in his other hand Love carries his arrow pointed at the dreamer's heart, and with it a branch of apple-blossom; as he reaches the bier, Love bends for a moment over Beatrice with the kiss which her lover has never given her; while the two green-clad dream-ladies hold the pall full of May-blossom suspended for an instant before it covers her face for ever." There are many minor incidents which need not detain us. Probably it was of the chalk drawing reproduced on page 63 which Mr. Rae bought of his friend in 1872 that Rossetti wrote "it was done right off at once."

It seems to be an elaborated study for the head of one of the "dream-ladies" and pall-bearers, who is on our right in this large picture. Its beauty speaks for itself. It is a more or less exact likeness of Miss Spartali, now Mrs. W. J. Stillman, and a distinguished lady-artist who sat otherwise to our painter, especially for the *Fiammetta* of a later date.

So long ago as 1855 our artist had been attracted by the subject of *Dante's Dream*, when he made a water-colour drawing to illustrate it, which Miss Heaton lent to the Burlington Club, 1883. Mr. V. Lushington wrote in the *Oxford and Cambridge Magazine*, August, 1866, an enthusiastic essay upon the design, which, in 1857, was included in the Russell Place Exhibition. A double predella was added to a smaller version of Rossetti's work, and it was the subject of countless discussions, experiments, and alterations, as well as of a world of studies and negotiations, including more than one change of owner. At last, in 1881, it was sold to Liverpool for £1,050, which was far below its artistic value, and less than Rossetti had received for much less ambitious examples of his art.

From the magnificent drawing in crayons Mr. Constantine A. Ionides lent, as No. 80, at the Burlington Club's exhibition of 1883, inscribed with the artist's monogram, and dated 1870, the reproduction of *A Lady with a Fan*, now before us, was taken. Like the models who sat for this masterpiece of style and many other fine things of the same category, its noblest function is to "live and be beautiful." Accordingly, it explains itself, and has no history that can be set forth here, except so far as relates to Rossetti's honour as, when he was pleased to do justice to himself, a perfect draughtsman. This exquisite example attests that no one could draw a head with more skill, art, and taste than he; while, except the hands, which are a little too large, the whole work is faultless. The year 1870 did not witness the completion of any important painting, a shortcoming for which the glorious *Proserpine*, that had its inception in a drawing of Mrs. Morris, dated 1871, made ample amends. Although the oil picture of this theme, which Mr. W. A. Turner lent to the Manchester Exhibition in 1882, and as No. 86 to the Burlington Club in 1883, is dated 1877, I consider it under the earlier date. It represents at life-size, a single figure of Proserpine in Hades, holding in her hand the pomegranate, by partaking of which she precluded her

Lady with a Fan.

return to earth.¹ She is passing along a gloomy corridor in her palace, and, on the wall behind her, a sharply defined space of light has fallen. It is the cool, bluish, silvery light of the moon, that because of some open door far overhead has penetrated the subterranean dimness, flashing down for a moment on the wall, revealing the ivy-tendrils that languish in the shade, displaying the queen, her features, the abundant masses of her hair, which seem to have become darker than was ever known on the earth above, and the sorrowfulness of her face. It shows also the slowly curling smoke of an incense-burner (the attribute of a goddess) which, in the still air of the gallery, circles upwards, and spreading, vanishes. Proserpine is clad in a steel-blue robe, that fits loosely her somewhat slender, slightly wasted, but noble frame of antique mould. It seems that she moves slowly with moody eyes instinct with slowly burning anger; yet she is outwardly still, if not serene, and very sad in all her stateliness; too grand for complaint. In these eyes is the deep light of a great spirit, and, without seeing or heeding, they look beyond the gloom before her. Her fully-formed lips, purplish now, but ruddy formerly, and once moulded by passion, are compressed, the symbols of a strenuous soul yearning for freedom, and, with all their pride, suffering, rather than enjoying goddess-ship. The even-tinted cheeks are rather flat; the face, so wide is the brow, is almost triangular, the nose like that of a grand antique. These features are set in masses of bronze-black and crimped hair, darkly lustrous as it is, that encompasses the head, and flows like an abundant mantle over her shoulders and bust. The wonder of the picture is in the face. The light cast on the wall throws the head in strong relief; she turns slowly towards the distant gleam; the ivy branch curves downwards, and assists, with the swaying lines of the drapery, the composition of the whole.²

[1] In countless early Italian pictures the bitten pomegranate is a well understood emblem of sorrow and pain. Hence it often occurs in the hand of the Infant Christ, who, in several examples, presses the fruit to the lips of His mother. On this account, no doubt, Rossetti placed the pomegranate in the hand of Proserpine.

[2] See the *Athenæum*, 1875, No. 2494. Rossetti wrote to Mr. Rae—"Oct 12th, 1877. The present one [*Proserpine*] belonging to myself was begun before Leyland's [of 1873], and thus had the immense advantage of the first inspiration from nature. It is unquestionably the finer of the two, and is the very flower of my work. . . . You

Rossetti wrote a sonnet in Italian, and an English version of the same, both of which are inscribed on the frame of the picture in question. The latter is as follows:

PROSERPINA.

"Afar away the light that brings cold cheer
   Unto this wall,—one instant and no more
   Admitted at my distant palace door.
Afar the flowers of Enna from this drear
Dire fruit, which, tasted once, must thrall me here.
   Afar those skies from this Tartarean gray
   That chills me: and afar, how far away,
The nights that shall be from the days that were.

"Afar from mine own self I seem, and wing
   Strange ways in thought, and listen for a sign:
   And still some heart unto some soul doth pine,
(Whose sounds mine inner sense is fain to bring,
Continually together murmuring,)—
   'Woe's me for thee, unhappy Proserpine!'"

These are indeed profound sighs, worthy of a goddess of the antique mould, and even sadder than the picture to which they refer. As to their subject, every friend of the painter knew that he was prouder of having invented it than of his share in devising, or rather applying to art any other theme in which he excelled. Reckoning *The Bride* as his technical *chef-d'œuvre*, I place *Proserpine* next to it, not because it is as well or better painted than half-a-dozen of his capital pieces, severally, but on account of the complete originality of its theme. On the other hand it should be remembered that, while he produced at least four or five versions of *Proserpine*, he never ventured on a second *Bride*.

The disastrous use of chloral, which was ultimately to insure his ruin, while it certainly did not act alone in promoting that catastrophe, had not, in 1873, although he became addicted to it more than two years

---

may perhaps have seen an article in the *Athenæum* relating to some pictures of mine completed at that time, and among which this is the first mentioned. The size is the same as Leyland's, the price 1,000 guineas." Mr. Leyland's version was sold in May, 1892, for 540 guineas; it was No. 314 at the Academy, 1883. Mr. Turner's version is that which Mr. W. Rossetti distinguishes as No. 3 of the rather numerous category of *Proserpines*; it now belongs to Mr. C. Butler, and is that which the painter himself thought highest of. It is the original of the plate before us for which we are indebted to Mr. Fairfax Murray.

before, made deep inroads upon our poet's energies, nor reduced his power in art. But it is noteworthy that, some time before 1871, when chloral came to his hands, nearly all the subjects of his pen and brush were more or less desponding ; of those none is sadder than *Proserpine*. At this time the chivalric and romantic subjects he had affected so late as the *Tristram and Iseult* of 1867, disappeared from his repertory, and gave place to the woe of Ceres' daughter, the mournful despair of *La Pia*, the sad pity of the *Donna della Finestra*, the ominous agony of *Pandora*, the sorrowing of Dante in the *Dream*, and the vague melancholy of *Veronica Veronese*, whose music is a dirge. Rossetti was not the man to "be sad o' nights out of mere wantonness," and therefore we must seek a cause for his selecting themes so gloomy and so woebegone as these, and may perhaps find it in the insidious effects of the drug which precipitated, though it did not cause his downfall, and—long before he had reached the allotted goal of man's existence—left desolate that noble "House of Life," whose inner treasures his poetry and painting set forth with

"Such a pencil, such a pen."

Besides the works described above, the years 1871, 1872, and 1873 were chiefly devoted by Rossetti to the production of minor portraits and new versions of already completed masterpieces, such as the repetitions of *Beata Beatrix*, *Hesterna Rosa*, *Rosa triplex*, and *Proserpine*. Two noteworthy exceptions are *Veronica Veronese*, which he painted for Mr. Leyland, and *La Ghirlandata*, which Mr. W. Graham bought. The former belongs to 1872, and, when it was No. 295 at the Academy in 1883, was thus described by the *Athenæum* in a criticism which I cannot now improve. "*Veronica Veronese* is the life-size figure in profile to our right, her head turned in a dreamy mood towards us, while with levelled eyelids and parted lips, she listens to the notes produced by her fingers on the strings of a violin hanging above the table where she has been writing music. The sharp notes are repeated, and inspired by the shrill song of a canary in a cage suspended behind the lady's seat, and to which she is endeavouring to give pathetic expression in the ordered music of her instrument. Rossetti appears here again to be giving expression in art to those associations of sound, colour, and sense which are hardly less obviously embodied in many pictures we have previously mentioned. The type chosen for the face is the most sculpturesque of all those he affected, and this picture is the most perfect illustration of it. Chromatically speaking, the work is almost classic in its style. The sumptuous, deep-toned greens of her sleeves accord with the grayer greens of the hangings behind the lady's figure; the tawny gold of her hair encloses clear-cut features of Miss Wilding's type, the carnations of which, although not wan, are but little tinged with the rose, and suggest a life of studious retirement and majestic leisure. The brightness of the music sheet repeats the tonality of the flesh tints, the jonquils on the table are adapted to the colour of the bird. In the like manner the tone and colour schemes of the whole example were constructed in harmonies, and on what may be called musical principles. The general aspect of the picture is that of a Paolo Veronese with the addition of searching execution, or an elaborately-finished Sebastiano which time had not lowered in lighting, tone or tint. This instance of *La Veronica* justifies the motto from the imaginary 'G. Ridolfi,' '*C'était le mariage des voix de la nature et de l'âme, l'aube d'une création mystique.*' It is one of the last of Rossetti's works of which music suggests the theme." Such is the masterpiece, in the firm and sculpturesque touch of which, as well as in its logical treatment and poetic inspiration, we recognize no sign of decaying powers or weakened will; such is the example the artist called " the fiddle-picture," which at Mr. Leyland's sale fetched a thousand guineas.

Mr. Graham's *La Ghirlandata* (R. A., 1883, No. 298) may fairly take its place with *Dis Manibus*, *The Bride*, and *Lilith*, without being compared with any of them. It shows the green-clad Lady of the Garlands sitting among the golden foliage of a thorn tree and myrtle copse; her hands are drawing music from a harp beside her seat, and her face proved her soul to be absorbed in the sound she produces. On either side, over her shoulders, an angel looks from between the glowing upper leaves of the copse, as if Heaven itself waited upon her song. Round the summit of the harp is slung a garland of roses and honeysuckles, the sweetest of earthly flowers, and the sky above, where the day of earth is dying, hints in its calm, ardent depths of a sweetness still beyond. The evening breeze has just risen and begins to lift the light drapery above her shoulders. In colour, this picture is chiefly a study of green, interspersed with blue of various shades—the deep blue aconite which appears at the base of the composition, the bright bird that flits through the trees, the wing pattern painted on the instrument, and the colour fading from the sky. These hues are balanced by the golden bronze of the lady's hair and the dusky-coloured harp, an instrument which is solid, with strings on each side.[1]

It appears that it was late in 1873 the first idea was suggested to Rossetti of illustrating with a picture his own poem *The Blessed Damozel*, which had originally appeared in the second number of the *Germ*, February, 1850. With this date therefore—although the first of several versions, that bought by Mr. W. Graham, was not available till the following year, while Mr. Leyland's picture had not the final touches till 1879—our illustrations of this stupendous work, are placed here. The picture more particularly illustrates a portion of the poem which appeared in the Tauchnitz edition of Rossetti's works, 1873, and is less known to English readers than either of the other versions. The legend, if such it can be called, which is entirely of the poet-painter's invention, tells us that the "Damozel," dying in the fulness of youth, and before her lover, waited for his coming in Heaven, while her earthly companions, maids and men, were united in perfect bliss. Time passed, and still the lover came not, but she continuously waited :—

> "It was the rampart of God's house
> That she was standing on ;
> By God built over the sheer depth
> The which is Space begun ;
> So high, that looking downward thence
> She scarce could see the sun.

---

[1] See the *Athenæum*, No. 2494, for the above, and further notes on Rossetti's pictures. Mr. W. Rossetti, the painter's brother, wrote that the flowers prominent in this work are, he thought, larkspurs, though the painter meant to depict monkshood, which is poisonous, and thus intended to suggest this in "Beauty which must die." This intention was not apparent to me in *La Ghirlandata*. My friend adds that, although the artist gave us so many pictures in which the pathetic as well as the poetic qualities of music are illustrated with the rarest subtlety, as of music that "overtakes far thought," he knew nothing of that art as such, and hardly cared to listen to its graver exercises.

* * * *

"Beneath, the tides of day and night
    With flame and darkness ridge
The void, as low as where this earth
    Spins like a fretful midge.

"Around her, lovers, newly met
    'Mid deathless love's acclaims,
Spoke evermore among themselves
    Their rapturous new names;
And the souls mounting up to God
    Went by her like thin flames.

"And still she bowed herself and stooped
    Out of the circling charm;
Until her bosom must have made
    The bar she leaned on warm,
And the lilies lay as if asleep
    Along her bended arm.

"From the fixèd place of Heaven she saw
    Time like a pulse shake fierce
Through all the worlds. Her gaze still strove
    Within the gulf to pierce
Its path; and now she spoke as when
    The stars sang in their spheres.

"The sun was gone now; the curled moon
    Was like a little feather
Fluttering far down the gulf; and now
    She spoke through the still weather.
Her voice was like the voice the stars
    Had when they sang together.

* * * *

"'I wish that he were come to me,
    For he will come,' she said.
'Have I not prayed in Heaven?—on earth,
    Lord, Lord, has he not pray'd?
Are not two prayers a perfect strength?
    And shall I feel afraid?'"

Thus yearning, the Damozel prefigures to herself the meeting she craves.

"'We two,' she said, 'will seek the groves
    Where the Lady Mary is,

> With her five handmaidens, whose names
>   Are five sweet symphonies,
> Cecily, Gertrude, Magdalen,
>   Margaret and Rosalys.
>
> "Circlewise sit they, with bound locks
>   And foreheads garlanded ;
> Into the fine white cloth like flame
>   Weaving the golden thread,
> To fashion the birth-robes for them
>   Who are just born, being dead.'"

The Blessed Damozel of this picture is of life-size, or a little larger, and, from amid a mass of blooming celestial roses, leans forward on one arm against and over the golden wall or parapet of Heaven, which is enriched with strange sculptures, and gleams in the mystical light of the place. Her loose and ample robe, of a pale cerulean blue, covers her shoulders, and, above this is a scarf of bronze tint, intermixed with silvery hues. The great heavenly lilies of sainthood lie in the hollow of her other arm. Her head is bent forward, and her pure pale face is marked with a love-yearning look in the never-weary, yet wistful eyes, and on her half-open lips sits immovably patient expectation ; her hair is of a deep golden tint, there are purple stars about it, and it seems to flow from under these upon her shoulders and her back in an abundant mass richly lighted. The exaltation of the soul which is expressed by the poem has been made concrete in the features, verifying the charm of the verses :

> "The wonder was not yet quite gone
>   From that still look of hers ;
> Albeit, to them she left, her day
>   Had counted as ten years."

The still dignity of her attitude is a masterpiece of graceful design, and the lines of the figure are amply supported by the subsidiary elements yet to be described, for the minor incidents of the work confirm the suggestions of the poem.

Behind the Damozel are the large mazes of the heavenly garden, where, under the branches of an enormous tree, numerous re-united lovers, clad in deep blue, are joyfully embracing, and are seen in changing lights and shadows. In front of the golden parapet, and bearing green palms

with which to welcome the lover for whose coming they, like the Damozel
wait, are two ministering spirits, both beautiful, but with different expres-
sions on their faces, the one more pitiful and sad than the other, for the

Sancta Lilias, so called, which was founded on The Blessed Damozel.

latter is younger, and his look is less sorrowful Their intensely blue
wings, instinct with latent fires, arch grandly over their heads, as if ready
to be expanded in flight, and launch the palm-bearers forth on the

celestial road by which all anticipate the lovers coming. Between these two ministers, and immediately below the shining parapet, appears a seraph, an infant's head surrounded by multiform and manifold wings like those of the tetramorph, and of a deep and vivid green; the face of this presence has a watchful and sad expression; it is the countenance of a Fate presaging sorrow and loss even in its steadfast regard and fixed lines.[1]

The *Blessed Damozel* is represented here by a reproduction of Rossetti's original design in chalk of a group of "lovers newly met," who appear in the background of Mr. Graham's version of the picture, not in that which Mr. Leyland had. A predella obtains with both examples, although they differ in various details. Several studies of this kind were dispersed at the Rossetti sale, 1883. The same picture is likewise represented by the cut of a work incorrectly named *Sancta Lilias*, which was the property of the late Lord Mount-Temple, and executed in 1874 as the date upon it states. It is a variation, in part, of the bust, hands and head, of the chief figure in the great picture, adapted to suit a differing expression and manner, and named according to the lilies in the maiden's hand. The robe and the background are golden. It was No. 87 at the Burlington Club Exhibition, 1883, where No. 84 was a similar study, belonging to Mr. W. Graham, in red chalk, and holding a palm. A study in red chalk of *Sancta Lilias* was Lot 35 at the Rossetti sale, and dated in the catalogue as of 1879.

Four works distinguished Rossetti's output in art during the year 1875. They are, besides "versions" and portraits as before, *Venus Astarte*, *The Sphinx*, or *The Question*, *Dis Manibus*, and *La Bella Mano*. The first of these, sometimes called *Astarte Syriaca*, a mystically inspired version of Mrs. W. Morris's lineaments, was illustrated by an admirable plate in the *Portfolio* of 1892, the immediate original of which was a chalk drawing, and an historical essay by the present writer. The second example is represented here by a reduction of a pencil drawing, the only one which Rossetti made to carry out an idea of what his biographer calls (in this I cannot agree with him) "one of my brother's most important inventions; he wished," says that loyal critic, "to carry it out as a picture, but found no feasible opportunity for doing

---

[1] See the *Athenæum*, 1877, No. 2581.

so. On his death-bed he composed two sonnets, as yet unpublished, to illustrate the same idea. In this design the Sphinx represents the mystery of existence, or the destiny of man, unfathomable by himself. Three personages—a youth, a man of mature age, and an old man—are shown as coming to the secret haunt of the Sphinx, to consult her as to the

Two Figures Embracing, from The Blessed Damozel.

arcana of Fate. The man is putting his question; the graybeard toils upward towards the spot; the youth, exhausted by his journey, sinks and dies, unable so much as to give words to the object of his quest. With upward and inscrutable eyes the Sphinx remains impenetrably silent." [1]

[1] The fraternal biographer continues, "It may be worthy of mention that, in representing the dying stripling, Rossetti was thinking of the premature fate of Oliver Madox

La bella Mano belonged to Mr. F. S. Ellis, who lent it to the Academy in 1883, No. 35. Here, the Lady with the Fine Hands, is washing them at a cistern and basin of brass, while two white-robed and red-winged Loves are in attendance, one holding the towel in readiness, the other having on a silver tray the adornments for her "bella mano." A mirror behind her head reflects the room and bed; these elements are deep in tone; a fire is burning in the chimney nook. The pictorial object of the work is to show the brilliancy of flesh tints, or carnations and whites relieved on a ground subdued to the eye, and yet everywhere replete with varied colour and material. In these respects the work is a marvel of art, the whole glowing in rich light, and being intensely deep in tone, and wealthy in colour. The sentiment of the design, as in most of Rossetti's pictures, lies in the face, and is discoverable in the light of a woman's hope, which fills the eyes, and has given a warmer rose tint to the full and slightly parted lips, that are red in their vitality. The face is slightly raised, and put sideways towards us, the figure standing in profile, so that the masses of deep golden hair which project from her brow, cast shadows on her upper features.

Dis Manibus, or *The Roman Widow*, I describe from notes made in Rossetti's studio in 1875, and published in the *Athenæum* of that year, soon after it was finished. The title here suggests the subject, that of a Roman widow seated in the funeral vault of her family, beside her husband's cinerary urn, the inscription on which is headed by the invariable words "Dis Manibus." She, as in some classical examples, is playing on two harps an elegy "To the Divine Manes" of the departed. She is robed in white, the mourning of noble ladies in Rome. The antique forms of the harps are rendered in tortoiseshell chiefly, with

---

Brown, a youth of singular promise, both as painter and as writer, who ended his brief life of less than twenty years in the November of 1874—a bitter grief to his father, Rossetti's life-long friend, Ford Madox Brown. This design Rossetti characteristically wrote of as being meant to be a sort of painted *Cloud Confines* (the name will be recognized as that of one of his poems). "I don't know," he added, "whether it would do to paint, being moonlight." The *Sphinx* seems to me an intractable subject, and to be overloaded with trite allegory that is unworthy of the inventor of so many subtleties, while the design, as such, is inferior and confused, and therefore, apart from the moonlight which would have to be dealt with, I am convinced that it would not "do to paint."

fillings of ebony or dark horn embossed in silver. She is seated right fronting us, and leans a little sideways to our left. On this side one of

The Sphinx.

the harps is reared on the arm of the bench, its horns are twined with pale wild roses, and beneath the urn is trained a festoon of garden roses. About the urn is bound the widow's wedding girdle of silver, dedicated to the dead or to the living husband. The second harp is on the bench on her left; her lean pale fingers seem to stray "preluding" a mournful strain upon the strings of the instruments, and her very eyes seem to listen; her lips we might expect would part and emit a faint funereal hymn. The moment chosen must be supposed to belong to one of those special occasions when the Romans solemnized mortuary rites, and which recurred at intervals during the year. The key colour of this picture is warm white, with a saffron hue; this obtained in the dress of the lady, and is varied by the less warm colour of the veil which swathes her head and throat, as well as by the intense pallor of the carnations. She has turned back the veil from her face so that we see the warm young features are sunken, a little pale, but still beautiful.

The Sea Spell, painted from Miss Wilding, and intended as a sort of companion to *Veronica Veronese*, for which she likewise sat, shows the Siren seated playing her lute, which is shadowed by the apple-tree and crowned with a rose-wreath. She is bending before the instrument which is upright before her; over her head is a white bird, attracted by the music and rushing through the air to listen to it. Behind are glimpses of the sunlit ocean and a blue firmament, vividly lighted. The witch is with abstracted eyes listening to her own music, and the vague charm of her ruddy lips seems to attest that she, urged by Fate, wove the enchantment that brought mariners to ruin, while she swings her body to the chanted cadence. Rossetti's sonnet illustrating this picture [1] begins

> "Her lute hangs shadowed on the apple tree
>   While flashing fingers weave the sweet-strung spell
> Between its chords."

The portrait of *Miss Christina Rossetti*, which is the last of our illustrations, belongs to the one brother, to whom we are indebted for it as well as for the plate after *Lilith*, and was drawn by the other brother of the lady whose choice verses have been, like so many pearls in a carcanet, strung in various editions of her poems. It will therefore be trebly welcome to the reader. It was drawn with coloured crayons, and with great care, in 1877; in 1883 it appeared as No. 43 at

---

[1] The *Sea-Spell*, which belonged to Mr. Leyland, and was sold with the rest of his pictures in May, 1892, for 420 guineas, was dated 1877, and exhibited at the Burlington Club in 1883.

the Burlington Club's exhibition of Rossetti's pictures, drawings, and studies. It attests that Time had not effaced from the lady's face the likeness of the Virgin in "*Ecce Ancilla Domini!*" of 1849, and it remains

Christina Rossetti.

the best portrait of our poet-painter's devoted and constant sister, his refuge in dark and painful days which she shared with his mother and brother, and one of the attendants of his latest hours.

Those hours witnessed the removal from amongst us of one of the most splendid geniuses of which the English nation can boast. They arrived all too soon after the portrait of his sister was completed, that is in less than five years, during which period Rossetti finished some less important works, replicas and new versions of several which have been mentioned in this text, and began certain examples which he did not live to complete. This is besides a large completed oil-picture, called *The Day Dream*. He had the great satisfaction of knowing that his fame as a poet was prodigiously extended by means of *Ballads and Sonnets*, published in September, 1881, while the sale in the same month of his *Dante's Dream* to the Liverpool Gallery affirmed that his honours as a painter would lose nothing in the future. It would have increased his happiness could he have known that in a few years two of the most characteristic of his pictures would be added to the National Gallery. He died at Birchington, Kent, on the 9th of April, 1882, and was buried in the churchyard of that village. To his memory this text is one of the tributes of an old friend.

Beatrice and her Nurse.

INDEX

Academy, Royal, 9
Alfieri, Count, 6
"Alma Mater," 48
"Astarte Syriaca," 88

"Beata Beatrix," 62
"Beloved, The," 58, 60
"Bionda del Balcone, La," 74
Birchington, 94
"Blessed Damozel," 84
"Blue Bower," 70
"Blue Closet," 41
"Bocca Baciata," 53
"Borgia," 31
Boyce, Mr., 31
Browning, Robert, 26, 51
Bruges, 28
Burne-Jones, Sir E., 16, 47

Cary, Mr., 9
"Chapel before the Lists," 48
Charlotte Street, 7, 8
Cheyne Walk, 58
"Christmas Carol," 70
Cimabue, 32
Cleveland Street, 13, 16, 23
Cockerell, Mr. Pepys, 32
Collinson, James, 17
Colvin, Mr. Sidney, 70
Combe, Mrs., 34
Cyclographic Society, 16

"Damsel of the Sangrael," 43
"Dante's Dream," 77
"Dante on the Anniversary of Beatrice's Death," 34

"Death of Breuse sans Pitié," 48
Della Guardia, 6
Deverell, Walter, 35, 36
"Dis Manibus," 90

"Ecce Ancilla Domini!" 19, 21

"Faust," 42
Ferdinand I., 6
"Fight for a Woman," 70
"Found," 37
Fra Angelico, 22

"Galahad in the Chapel," 48
Gaujean, M., 24
"Genevieve," 9, 15, 16
Germ, The, 23, 25, 28, 31
"Giotto painting a Portrait of Dante," 32
Glass, Designs for Stained, 56
"Ghirlandata, La," 73, 83
Graham, Mr. William, 24, 75, 82, 83

Herbert, Miss, 68, 73
"Hesterna Rosa," 30
Heugh, Mr., 24
Hogarth Club, 49
Holbein, 22, 23
"How they met Themselves," 32
Hughes, Mr. Arthur, 29, 42
Hunt, Mr. Holman, 11, 12, 13, 14, 16, 18, 24, 37

"Johnson at the Mitre," 53

King's College, London, 7

King's College School, 8
Kirkup, Mr., 32

"La Bella Mano," 90
"Laboratory, The," 26
"Lady of Pity," 74
"Lady with the Fan," 78
"Lady with the Chain," 70
"Lancelot asleep before the Shrine of the San Grael," 46
"Lancelot escaping from the Chamber of Guinevere," 48
"Lancelot and Guinevere at the Tomb of Arthur," 40
Leathart, Mr. 38
"Lilith," 66
Llandaff Cathedral, the triptych at, 49
Louvre, The, 28
"Loving Cup," 70
"Lucrezia Borgia," 51
Lyell, Charles, 8

McCracken, Mr. 24, 34
Madox-Brown, 11, 12, 14, 19, 24, 28
Malta, 6
"Mary, the Girlhood of the Virgin," 15, 16, 18
Millais, Sir John, 9, 12, 14, 21, 28
"Monna Vanna," 70
Morris, Mr. William, 25, 41, 42, 43, 50, 78
    ,,   ,, Mrs. 88
Murray, Mr. Fairfax, 26

Naples, 6
Newman Street, 31
Nineveh, Burden of, 51

"Pandora," 74, 75,
"Paolo and Francesca, 39, 58
"Parable of Love," 31
"Passover in the Holy Family," 39
Patmore, Mr. Coventry, 16, 31
Paul, Rev. 8
Pierce, Miss, 6
Polidori, Gaetano, 6, 9

Polidori, Dr., 6
Pre-Raphaelite Brotherhood, 9, 12, 16, 17
"Princess Sabra drawing the fatal Lot," 74
"Proserpine," 78, 81

Rae, Mr. George, 41, 42, 43, 52, 56, 70
"Ramoscello, Il," 70
"Regina Cordium," 36, 70
Retzsch, 9
"Rosa triplex," 73
Rossetti, Miss Christina Georgina, 6, 19, 22, 92
   ,, Mrs. D. G. 56
   ,, Mrs. Frances Mary Lavinia, 6, 7, 19
   ,, Gabriele, 6, 7, 8
   ,, Miss Maria Francesca, 6
   ,, Mr. William Michael, 6, 17, 25
Ruskin, Mr. John, 39

"Sancta Lilias," 88
"Salutatio Beatricis," 50
"Sea Spell," 92
"Sibylla Palmifera," 64, 65
Siddall, Elizabeth Eleanor, 35, 36, 47
"Sister Helen," 51
"Sphinx," 89
Stolberg, Louisa of, Countess of Albany, 6
Stuart, Charles Edward, 6

Taylor, Sir Henry, 30
Tennyson, Lord, 40
Tintoret, 61
Tristram and Iseult, 70

Union at Oxford, 45

Vasto d'Ammone, 6
"Venus Verticordia," 66
"Veronica Veronese," 82

"Washing Hands," 69
"Wedding of St. George," 42
Wilding, Miss Alice, 70, 73, 74, 92
Woodward, Mr. 48
Woolner, Thomas, 17, 31,

www.ingramcontent.com/pod-product-compliance
Lightning Source LLC
Chambersburg PA
CBHW030051170426
43197CB00010B/1483